BOTTOMLESS
Cup

Learning to Live
from an
Endless Supply

Andrew A. Bauer

Unless otherwise indicated, scripture quotations are taken from the Holy Bible, NEW INTERNATIONAL VERSION®, NIV® Copyright © 1973, 1978, 1984, 2011 by Biblica, Inc.® Used by permission. All rights reserved worldwide. • Scripture quotations marked (ESV) are taken from The Holy Bible, English Standard Version® (ESV®), copyright © 2001 by Crossway, a publishing ministry of Good News Publishers. Used by permission. All rights reserved. • Scripture quotations marked (NASB) are taken from the New American Standard Bible®, Copyright © 1960, 1962, 1963, 1968, 1971, 1972, 1973, 1975, 1977, 1995 by The Lockman Foundation. Used by permission. • Scripture quotations marked (MSG) are taken from The Message. Copyright © by Eugene H. Peterson 1993, 1994, 1995, 1996, 2000, 2001, 2002. Used by permission of NavPress Publishing Group.

ISBN: 978-1-4866-1814-9

Word Alive Press
119 De Baets Street Winnipeg, MB R2J 3R9
www.wordalivepress.ca

WORD ALIVE
—P R E S S—

Cataloguing in Publication information can be obtained from Library and Archives Canada.

DEDICATION

My life and ministry have been shaped by many people, but two have influenced me more than any others. I would like to dedicate this book to my father, Albert Bauer, who left this world on November 19, 2009—far too early for those of us he left behind. My dad encountered Christ as a young husband and father, and from that time he lived his life full out for Jesus. I would also like to dedicate it to Pam, my wife of twenty-five years. She has been my rock and my best friend.

Contents

INTRODUCTION

Your Heavenly Father is neither a cup-half-full nor a cup-half-empty sort of person. He's a "cup overfloweth" sort of God (see Psalm 23). God doesn't want us to live and work for Him with barely enough energy, resources, or creativity to get through the day, let alone the week. He wants us to live with a bottomless cup.

I'm very particular about my coffee. My wife, Pam, calls me a "coffee snob." I prefer to say that I'm just passionate about my coffee. What's even better than a great cup of coffee is a great cup of coffee at a restaurant that offers a bottomless cup. As long as I'm drinking, they're pouring. I believe that's how God wants us to live. As long as we're loving and serving in the name of Jesus, we have access to an unlimited source of spiritual strength. But is that your experience? It hasn't always been mine.

It will be far more challenging to live this book than to write it or, I'm guessing, read it. I don't write with the credentials of a scholar, an expert, or someone who is exceptionally accomplished in this aspect of life. Rather,

I write as a stumbling fool who has happened upon a treasure in the field. By telling you about it, I'll have to share some of the treasure, but that won't lessen its value. There's a limitless supply!

The principles I share may seem to some like secret knowledge, and to others like waters of life. But to many they may seem simply like insanity. They're counter-intuitive and shouldn't make sense, but they work. They're like the "deeper magic" in C.S. Lewis' book *The Lion, The Witch, and The Wardrobe*—principles that hold sway stronger than those which seem to govern the world as we see it. When Lucy and Susan ask Aslan what it meant when he was resurrected and the stone table broken, he replied:

> It means ... that though the Witch knew the Deep Magic, there is a magic deeper still which she did not know. Her knowledge only goes back to the dawn of time. But if she could have looked a little further back, into the stillness and darkness before Time dawned, she would have read there a different incantation.[1]

If we could see past the way things seem to work in the natural realm to the spiritual principles God has put in place, we'd find a very different pattern for life—one that gives life rather than takes it, and one that feeds the soul rather than depletes it. A very "different incantation"! As

---

[1] C.S. Lewis, *The Lion, the Witch and the Wardrobe* (London: HarperCollins, 1998), 185.

we seek to live the Christ-life in this harsh and challenging world, at times it seems that we aren't getting the results we should be getting and that we're hitting a wall instead of meeting with success. Common sense tells us to ramp up our efforts. We need to try harder, strive more passionately, pray louder, be holier. We need to convince more people how right we are and get them to strive really hard with us! We need to go faster, go bigger, make more noise, strategize more intelligently, pay for a more expensive consultant. Sooner or later all of our efforts just have to pay off … at least that's what makes sense to many of us. We've shaped God in our image—an edgy, results-oriented manager who yells a lot. His main mottos are: "I'm disappointed in you" and "Try harder next time!"

Even as I write this, I'm haunted by the image of God as a driven, results-oriented manager of the universe who is unimpressed by me spending an afternoon eating Decadent chocolate chunk cookies, drinking coffee, reading, and listening to music when I ought to be producing volumes of material. I don't know what percentage of this twisted perception comes from our deceived human state, in which the god of this age blinds the minds of the unbelieving (i.e. those who don't take God at His word), or from my cultural conditioning in the Protestant/Puritan work ethic, which equates sweat and hard work with a godly life. More than likely it comes from my upbringing in a no-nonsense, blue-collar, get-the-job-done household with a father who had "driven-ness" issues of a whole different order. I'm uncomfortable with the possibility that God likes it when we occasionally unplug from responsibility and enjoy life. I know there are those with the opposite problem, who need to be reminded that they weren't born for the purpose of consuming pizza, holding down a couch, and conquering every level of the latest Halo game. But for those of us for whom productivity and performance have become the primary organizing principles of our lives, we need to hear the Master leading us out of the slavery of our Egypt and into a different way of life.

Consider the exchange between Martha and her sister Mary in Luke 10. Martha had some really good points. The meal needed to be prepared … it wasn't going to cook itself! The table needed to be set. Things needed to be done. It would appear that Jesus wasn't tuned-in to the needs of the guests, and certainly not to what it took to prepare a meal of that magnitude! Jesus' response to Martha's insistent plea was counter-intuitive, yet if Martha didn't hear and respond accordingly, she would miss the most important learning moment of her life. There was something more important than getting the job done, something more important than what might seem like the obvious first priority. Martha needed to learn to serve from a place of rest. What a difference it would make to serve with a peace-filled heart, carried along by the joy of the Master's presence, instead of being worried and upset by many things. (We'll re-visit Martha and Mary later.)

I'm talking about the principles of rest and trust, of living a life of continual dependence on the Lord. It doesn't always make sense, but if you can unlock the secrets of living this way, you'll be set free from insecurities, worry, and the fear that comes from feeling like you're in way over your head and at any moment you could be exposed as one who just doesn't measure up. (Okay, maybe that's just me.)

If I still have your attention, I'd like to invite you to journey with me as I discover a way of living that Jesus intended for us all along. He wants us to live with a bottomless cup, an inexhaustible source of strength and power, and a passion and vision for the things He has called us to do. He never meant for His church to be worn out, burnt over, frustrated, exhausted, disillusioned, guilt-ridden, and resentful. If we are, we've missed the point and are living life differently than He ever intended.

One night after a weekend of special meetings at our church, I took the guest speaker out for a late supper. We went to a great restaurant that served wood-fired pizza, and we talked about our experiences in life and ministry. It can be as rare as a water cooler in the desert to find someone with whom you feel safe enough to share the challenges of pastoral ministry, so we nursed our pizza for hours and kept the glasses of Coke coming. I assumed they were free refills, as was the policy of most restaurants in the area. That wasn't one of my brightest moments. When I got the bill at the end of the night, I realized I had surpassed my resources much earlier in the evening. How many times in life do I surpass my physical and emotional resources before I even realize it? I always ask if the drinks are bottomless now. I've also learned how to recognize when I'm living outside of the limitless provision of my Heavenly Father and the gift of the Spirit He so graciously gives. The sooner I recognize my barren self-sufficiency, the sooner I can get back to my bottomless cup.

I've been in an empty place many times, and chances are so have you. What are we missing? I believe the answer to this question, although found in many places throughout the Bible, is beautifully and poignantly summarized in Matthew 11:25–30:

> At that time Jesus said, "I praise you, Father, Lord of heaven and earth, because you have hidden these things from the wise and learned, and revealed them to little children. Yes, Father, for this was what you were pleased to do. All things have been committed to me by my Father. No one knows the Son except the Father, and no one knows the Father except the Son and those to whom the Son chooses to reveal him. Come to me, all you who are weary and burdened, and I will give you rest. Take my yoke upon you and learn from me, for I am gentle and humble in heart, and you will find rest for your souls. For my yoke is easy and my burden is light."

Many of you have read this passage of scripture so many times, you could almost quote the last couple of verses. Perhaps you were made to commit them to memory in some kind of youth group memory verse contest, like I was. Why don't you stop, go back, and read them once more? I know you probably skimmed them because they're so familiar. I would have. They're familiar, but maybe too familiar. Dust off the words and take a fresh look at them. What do they really mean?

As we'll discuss in the chapters to follow, I believe that Jesus is extending an invitation—not just to take a vacation or a break from our efforts so that we can throw ourselves into them even more fully once we've rested, but rather to do it all differently. I believe Jesus is telling us that if we live with a bottomless cup, we won't become weary and heavy-burdened, needing to be rescued from burn-out.

Is this kind of life truly possible, or am I just teasing you? I'm still in pursuit of it myself, but I don't believe that Jesus would invite us to something that was entirely unattainable. His promises can be trusted. We're told in 2 Peter 1:3 that: "*His divine power has given us everything we need for a godly life through our knowledge of him …*" He has already provided everything we need to live godly in this world. All the resources necessary for life are ours, continually … kind of like a bottomless cup. We just need to learn how to access them. Can it be that simple? Let's see …

Chapter One
A NEW VIEW OF LIFE

"… no one knows the Father except the Son and anyone to whom the Son chooses to reveal him."
(Matthew 11:27b)

My idea of God is a not divine idea.
It has to be shattered from time to time.
He shatters it Himself. He is the great iconoclast.
Could we not almost say that this shattering is
one of the marks of His presence?
—C.S. Lewis[2]

Often in human conversation, we weigh the importance of someone's statement by the way in which they lead up to it. I remember the night I proposed to my wife. I'd been planning it for about three weeks, and she had no idea it was about to happen. She was working for the summer in a city two thousand kilometres away,

[2] C.S. Lewis, *A Grief Observed* (London: Faber, 1966), 52.

and I flew down to see her. I'd planned the whole evening very carefully—from the restaurant I chose, to the walk we would take after dinner, to the location and content of our conversation. All were part of a carefully planned preamble to one of the most important questions I would ever ask. When I got down on one knee, the importance of the words became very clear.

Have you ever been in a discussion and someone says, "Can I ask you a question?"? You know that whatever is coming is serious, as they've just used up breath to ask the privilege of asking another question. Or what about those moments when someone says, "I have something to tell you, and I don't know how to say it"? They probably know exactly how to say it, but it's so serious, they have to prepare themselves and you.

When Jesus starts talking in Matthew 11:25, He gives a preamble before voicing these often-quoted words in verses 28–30. You likely don't remember the preamble, and if you've read it, you've probably skimmed over it to get to the "really good stuff." Let's take a look at what He says here, as it will enhance our understanding of the significance of the passage as a whole.

> At that time Jesus declared, "I thank you, Father, Lord of heaven and earth, that you have hidden these things from the wise and understanding and revealed them to little children; yes, Father, for such was your gracious will. All things have been handed over to me by my Father, and no one knows the Son except the

Father, and no one knows the Father except the Son
and anyone to whom the Son chooses to reveal him."
(Matthew 11:25–27, ESV)

At first glance, it may be difficult to understand the connection between these words and what follows. We need to understand that Jesus wasn't sent into this world as the Son of God just to die as a sacrifice for the sins of humanity—although that was a significant part of His mission—but to also bring us a greater revelation of the Father.

A NEW REVELATION

When Jesus arrived on the scene, He found a lot of extremely religious people—many of them well intentioned, and some of them less so—who had missed the point entirely. They were working hard to impress a God they didn't understand, and they were killing themselves doing things He'd never asked them to do. They'd hitched their wagon to the wrong star—an imposter star that was going nowhere.

Rigorous religious observance was the order of the day. The Pharisees were like the US Marines of religious observance. But for all of their diligent effort, they were far from the heart of God. Jesus says of them in Matthew 23:13–15:

But woe to you, scribes and Pharisees, hypocrites!
For you shut the kingdom of heaven in people's faces.
For you neither enter yourselves nor allow those
who would enter to go in. Woe to you, scribes and

> *Pharisees, hypocrites! For you travel across sea and land to make a single proselyte, and when he becomes a proselyte, you make him twice as much a child of hell as yourselves.* (ESV)

Jesus came to bring a revelation of the real heart of God. The Bible provides a progressive revelation of the nature and character of God. The books of the Old Testament, written by human authors under the inspiration of the Holy Spirit, serve as a lens through which we can see God more clearly. I got my first pair of glasses to correct my near-sightedness when I was twelve years old. I was standing in our dining room looking out the window when I put them on for the first time outside of the optometrist's office. When I slipped them onto my face, the tree across the road from our house suddenly leapt into focus. Where there had only been a green blob of colour, there were suddenly distinct leaves standing out clearer than I'd ever seen them, waving in the breeze. I didn't realize that I was seeing the tree incompletely until I put my glasses on and could see it clearly. As we read the Old Testament revelation, we get a glimpse of what God is like, but it's still like a blob of green.

In the Old Testament, God deals with the lives of the patriarchs in Genesis, leading them on wayward journeys to live out the promise He spoke over Abraham, often in spite of themselves. Then we see Him as a valiant warrior fighting to set His people free from slavery to the Egyptian empire. Under Moses, Joshua, and the judges, He teaches and disciplines this new nation of people to obediently follow the path He has commanded for them. As the Israelite nation continually falls into pursuit of the gods of the nations around them, God shows Himself through the prophets as the faithful lover pursuing an unfaithful people.

But it's when Jesus comes on the scene in the gospels that God suddenly comes into focus. Jesus is theology at its best. We see most clearly in the incarnate Son the motivations, priorities, and values of the Father. Jesus came to bring an undiluted revelation of the heart of God to humanity. In this passage, Jesus announces that He desires to show a new facet of the nature of God and how He wants to relate to humankind. This new way helps us see God not as demanding something from us that we could never give, but rather as a loving Father who first provides for us everything He requires.

THE HEARTS OF THE HEARERS

Jesus' preamble in Matthew 11 alerts us to the fact that what He is about to say is a revelation that only can be grasped by those with pure hearts and simple trust. Those who truly want to know God will hear the message behind the message. They will understand what Jesus is really saying: "God is not the angry, miserable, impossible-to-please ogre you think He is. He's not driving you to a performance-oriented exhaustion as you strive to please Him. He's not impressed with your self-righteous attempts at besting one another in heroic feats of rule-keeping. He longs for you to know Him, love Him, and trust Him. I want to show you a new path."

The words "*Come to me all you who labour*" aren't just a panic button promise for those in burnout. I know many people who have burnt themselves out with religious activity and then come across these words. Their reaction is often one of two things: either they respond in cynicism and anger because the words are so far from their experience that they're almost a cruel joke, or they respond with that misquoted and misapplied verse: "There's no rest for the wicked." They believe that the promise is for everyone else but them, that they aren't good enough or they didn't try hard enough. They then get back on the cruel carousel of religious effort.

Jesus' words are an invitation to those who have the humility to admit they've missed the point to repent and do life differently. He invites us to do life in a way that brings freedom, joy, and peace instead of slavery, guilt, and exhaustion.

Do you see yourself in these responses? Are you trapped in a religion of striving to please God, who you maybe imagine to be impatient and angry with you? Have you tried hard to serve Him yet find yourself resenting it more every day, wondering where the freedom, joy, and peace went that you thought you were promised? Maybe you're missing the point. Maybe there really is a better way to do this. Good! That means you're a candidate for a whole new revelation of God. Everything is about to change. You're the sort of person Jesus had in mind when He spoke these words. There's just one catch: you need to give up being so grown up, so wise and learned, and be willing to be like a child. Jesus stated that the Father hides these truths of the kingdom from the wise and learned and reveals them to little children.

LIKE LITTLE CHILDREN

We in the church tend to be answer people. We want everyone around us to think we know all the answers, we've got it all sorted out, and we don't need any help. We don't like mystery or unanswered questions. Over the years in church leadership, I've watched new believers come into the church and pick up on this quickly. They realize that it's not cool in church culture to not have a ready answer, even if it's a "pat" answer that isn't really honest or even theologically correct.

God is not nervous about mystery. He's not as concerned about answers as we are. In fact, He loves to keep a little bit of mystery in all that He does. He calls it wonder. He loves to see it in the eyes of a child when they see something for the first time. Wonder puts the "magic" in Christmas and makes a child squeal with delight at a carnival. Wonder helps us realize that there's something big and grand about life that we don't yet understand. There has to be someone much bigger, wiser, and more powerful than us who made all of this and holds it in His hand. I don't have all the answers, but I can trust that He does. Wonder is the opposite of cynicism, and you need some of it to see Jesus' revelation of the Father. The revelation is hidden from the wise and learned, but it's revealed to little children.

Children approach relationships with more trust than do adults. A child just trusts that when they jump off the stair landing into the waiting arms of their parent, that parent will catch them. It doesn't cross their mind that the parent will miss, or will turn at the last second and let them fall mercilessly to the ground. Nor do they spend a significant amount of time worrying about whether their parent picked up all the groceries they were supposed to. They just know that supper will be ready when it's supposed to be. Jesus said that we must receive the kingdom like a little child in order to enter it (Luke 18:17). I believe this is a question of trust. A child doesn't need to be convinced by lengthy debate and unquestionable proof that something is true. If someone in a trusted relationship says it's true, it's undoubtedly true!

The Christian faith isn't unreasonable but is filled with reasonable answers to its claims; however, it's not in its reason that we trust but in its resurrected Lord. At many points this faith must be believed to be seen, which is difficult for many adult-minded people. What Jesus is about to share cannot be accepted by people who have to first understand it. It has to be believed, and then the understanding will follow.

Do you want to see what God is really like? Do you want to see the life He's planned for you? Then you'll need to turn in your cynicism for a dose of wonder. You'll need to approach Him in a new way. Forget all the answers you thought you knew. Lay down all the great achievements you've notched on your Bible belt. Stop being the answer person you think you need to be and step into a place of mystery, where God can be different than the image of Him you've created in your mind.

C.S. Lewis refers to God as "the great iconoclast." An iconoclast is someone who destroys idols, and God has an amazing way of shattering our idols. We tend to create an image of God that usually says more about us than it does about Him. When we encounter Him in real, everyday ways, He's not as we expect Him to be.

When my oldest daughter, Carrie-Anne, was about ten years old, I walked into the living room one day when she was playing a high energy song called "Boomin'" by Toby Mac for her younger brother and sister. She had just turned up the volume a little bit and had this mischievous look on her face. I put out my hand for the remote with a look that said: "What do you think you're doing?" Her mischievous smile slumped into an "awww, busted" look. Then I did the unexpected and unthinkable—I cranked it about twice as loud. We both burst into laughter and jumped around the living room. (Some songs just need lots of volume.) That day, I totally shattered her preconception of her dad.

Some of us need our ideas of God shattered. Some of us need to laugh with our heavenly Father and jump around the living room. Jesus' contention with the Pharisees was that they spent all of their time studying the scriptures to gain a revelation of who God was, but they totally missed the point. They had shaped God into an angry being who demanded sour faces and intense rule-keeping and who had outlawed the enjoyment of life. Nothing upset Jesus more than people misrepresenting His Father as one who loads burdens on people's backs. Speaking of the teachers of the Law and the Pharisees, He said: "*They tie up heavy, cumbersome loads and put them on other people's shoulders, but they themselves are not willing to lift a finger to move them*" (Matthew 23:4).

Jesus came to give a greater revelation of the Father. He is God in the flesh. As we watch the life of Jesus unfold in the gospels, we see the most coherent and untarnished theology possible: a living theology. You want to know how God thinks? Listen to Jesus' teachings and parables. You want to know His priorities as He governs the universe? Watch Jesus pull an unclean woman out of a crowd and set her free from twelve years of agony. You want to know how He desires to connect with and love humanity? Watch Jesus forgive the people who are pounding nine-inch spikes into his wrists and feet.

When Jesus says that no one knows the Father except the Son and those to whom the Son chooses to reveal Him, I'm on the edge of my seat. I want to be one of those people. I want Jesus to reveal Father God to me so that I may truly know Him. If I've shaped God into an inaccurate image of who He truly is, I want to replace that idol with the one true God! I don't just want to know about Him properly … I want to know Him personally!

Jesus is getting ready to share a revelation of the Father that will alter our view of reality. If we can get this, we'll live differently. We'll no longer carry burdens we were never made to carry, or see God as angrily and impatiently waiting for us to get it right. We'll no longer live under the guilt of unfinished labours and unmet expectations from a God who is never satisfied with our efforts. We'll be set free to truly live.

Jesus said in John 10:10: "*The thief comes only to steal and kill and destroy; I have come that they may have life, and have it to the full.*" Why does trying to serve God sometimes feel more like being robbed than living in abundance? Is it possible we're doing it wrong? Is it possible there's another way Jesus tried to tell us about, but we missed it? Let's lean in closely, listen with fresh ears, and look with new glasses at what Jesus is saying to us.

Questions
FOR REFLECTION AND DISCUSSION

1. What are some assumptions about a co-worker or neighbour that were shattered when you really got to know them?

2. How could the Jewish teachers of the Law spend their lives studying the words of God yet develop so many incorrect assumptions about what God is like?

3. What words or actions of Jesus do you think religious people found most disturbing?

4. Is it possible that you have some misperceptions about God? How would you know if you did?

5. What would it look like in your life to approach God in a more childlike way?

Chapter Two
THE INVITATION

"Come to me, all you who are weary
and burdened ... "
(Matthew 18:28)

"A real conversation always contains an
invitation. You are inviting another person to
reveal herself or himself to you, to tell you who
they are or what they want."
—David Whyte[3]

There is something compelling about invitations. Even when you want to find a creative way to decline, there's something meaningful about being invited. It means someone sat down with a blank piece of paper to make a list, and your name came to their mind. After careful consideration, you made the cut. They thought

---

[3] David Whyte, "The Questions that Have No Right to Go Away," *Huffpost*, June 18. 2012, accessed March 4, 2019, https://www.huffingtonpost.com/2012/06/14/the-questions-that-have-n_n_1596931.html.

pleasant thoughts about you and wanted you to be there. Then they carefully selected the invitation cards to communicate just the right sentiment. Your name was written in beautiful script, and then double postage was paid so that your RSVP could be sent easily. Maybe the invitation came in the form of a phone call, text, or social network message. Either way, they had to look you up and considered you someone worth being with, someone they wanted close. An invitation says, "I want you here with me. Won't you come?"

Invitation also involves vulnerability. When I asked Pam out on our first date, my heart was pounding, my hands were clammy, and I had to talk past the lump in my throat. I knew she could very well turn me down. I was taking a risk. I'm glad I did, but in order to put out that invitation, I had to make myself vulnerable to rejection and embarrassment.

The theme of invitation is prevalent throughout scripture from Genesis to Revelation. The creator of the universe extends an invitation to people—to you and to me. That means you're on His mind. He has considered you and desires for you to come close and be with Him. He loves you enough to make Himself vulnerable. Almighty God, who could sneeze and destroy us all, humbles Himself to ask if we would do Him the honour of coming to Him.

As God walks in the garden in the cool of the day in Genesis 3, He knows what has happened. He knew it would happen before He created Adam, so He made provision for Adam's sin before the creation of the world

(1 Peter 1:20). As He walks in the garden, He calls the man to Himself. It was the first invitation, and since that moment, God's invitation to mankind has rung through the ages. He invites Noah into a covenant. He invites Moses, the murderer-shepherd, to lead His people; He repeatedly invites the people of Israel to trust and follow Him, despite multiple stubborn rejections. Hear some of the great invitation passages that echo in scripture.

Invitation to relational obedience:

> *...but if you return to me and obey my commands, then even if your exiled people are at the farthest horizon, I will gather them from there and bring them to the place I have chosen as a dwelling for my Name.* (Nehemiah 1:9)

God, in His kindness, extends an invitation to the people who had continually rebelled and turned away from Him, asking them to return and enjoy the fruit of obedience.

Invitation to conversation: "*Come now, let us reason together* ..." (Isaiah 1:18, ESV). God shows his willingness to indulge our need to understand with an invitation to make sense of the vastness of His mercy. He's not intimidated by our rebellion, nor does He feel the need to intimidate us. He rather invites us to consider the truth instead of our foolish imaginations.

Invitation to rich blessings of knowing the Lord: "*Come, all you who are thirsty, come to the waters ... come, buy and eat ... Seek the Lord...*" (Isaiah 55:1, 6a). God invites us to a banquet of blessing at His cost if we'll only abandon the folly of our selfishness and sin. It's just like God to wear us down with His kindness and love. In spite of His relentless pursuit of a wandering people, He continues to hold out this offer of true pleasures in His presence if we will come to Him.

Invitation to wholeness: "*Return, faithless people; I will cure you of backsliding*" (Jeremiah 3:22a). God not only offers amnesty for those who have broken trust with Him, but offers to bring them into spiritual healing so that they will no longer be susceptible to falling away. God blasts our illusion that by our great faith we render Him weak in the knees for us, as if some of us are more attractive than others. His invitation is not only to those of great faith, but to the faithless as well. He is weak at the knees for all of humanity.

Invitation to restoration and intimacy: "*Therefore I am now going to allure her* [Israel]; *I will lead her into the wilderness and speak tenderly to her. There I will give her back her vineyards, and will make the Valley of Achor a door of hope*" (Hosea 2:14–15a). God's invitation doesn't come in harsh demands but in the sweet wooing of a lover who just won't let go. In His invitation, He wants to not only convince your mind but your heart as well.

Invitation to revival: "*'Even now,' declares the Lord, 'return to me with all your heart, with fasting and weeping and mourning*" (Joel 2:12). It's never too late. If we're willing to recognize the depth of our betrayal in spurning the God who loved us, and then repent and turn back to Him, He will give us new life.

Invitation to new destiny: "*'Come, follow me,' Jesus said, 'and I will send you out to fish for people*" (Matthew 4:19). Jesus invited the twelve apostles to be with Him (Mark 3:14). He not only wanted followers, or students, but He desired to set these men on a path to a new destiny. Their lives would no longer be simply about catching and cleaning fish, although they may still do that from time to time, but about bringing the life of Heaven to people who were dead inside. They would shape other destinies and, ultimately, the history of the world.

Invitation to adventure: "*'Come,' he said. Then Peter got down out of the boat, walked on the water and came toward Jesus*" (Matthew 14:29). Jesus invites us out of the ordinary, out of life as usual, to a life where anything can and will happen. The life of following Jesus, of being carried by the wind of the Spirit of God, isn't intended to be boring or for the faint of heart. It's an invitation to the best life there is—to a life of faith, courage, and honour— the very things the human heart was made for.

Invitation to dinner: "*Here I am! I stand at the door and knock. If anyone hears my voice and opens the door, I will come in and eat with that person, and they with me*" (Revelation 3:20). This verse paints one of the most beautiful pictures in scripture (next to Hosea 1–3) of God's vulnerability, as He risks rejection by the hearts of humanity. Jesus stands at the door of every human heart and knocks. His desire is to be so close, so intimate with each person that He literally lives within us and we break bread with the creator of the universe and Saviour of our souls. But we must respond to the invitation by opening the door. Still He knocks.

Invitation to revelation:

After this I looked, and there before me was a door standing open in heaven. And the voice I had first heard speaking to me like a trumpet said, "Come up here, and I will show you what must take place after this." (Revelation 4:1)

God wants to reveal His will and purpose to those who love Him: "*Call to me and I will answer you and tell you great and unsearchable things you do not know*" (Jeremiah 33:3). John was invited into a special opportunity to see things that none of us will see or fully understand until we leave this world for the next, but all through scripture we see that God loves to talk with and reveal Himself to those who will listen.

These are just a few of the passages in scripture that communicate God's invitation to us. He is a God of invitation. It's not okay with God that we are separated from Him, held hostage by the power of sin. That's why He planned a "sting operation" to invade this earth by the presence of His Son, Jesus. That's why He was willing to pay such a phenomenal price for our forgiveness and freedom. That's why His love bent so low, and that's why He continues to bend so low for every human soul, inviting us into His love.

WHICH INVITATION WILL YOU ACCEPT?

In our passage, Jesus not only invites the weary and burdened to "come" but to "come to me." Often we know that we can't do it on our own and that we need help, but we go looking in other places instead of looking to the one who is our source!

Consider the following parable: His little girl's eighth birthday was approaching quickly. The father wanted to present her with a dollhouse made by his own hands that she could play with and remember for the rest of her life. He worked late at night, week after week, to complete the gift on time. It was a work of art and a labour of love—every post for the banister in the stairwell carefully shaped, every piece of furniture crafted with skill. The finest of detail was painted on the walls of each room. The night before her birthday he put the finishing touches on the front door.

The effort had the desired effect. When the wrapping was peeled away and she got her first glimpse of the dollhouse, the eight-year-old girl squealed with delight, as only eight-year-old girls can. She loved the gift and began playing with it before all the paper was even off.

Knowing his daughter's love of the outdoors, the father had only one warning for her: "This is a very special gift that Daddy worked hard to make, so don't take your dollhouse outside." Despite her love of dolls, she was a real tomboy, so he knew she'd need the reminder.

"Okay," she said distractedly.

A few days later on the Saturday afternoon, the little girl didn't hear anyone else moving around in the house.

She thought the sandbox would be a great place to play with her dollhouse, so she quietly took it out the side door and had a wonderful time playing with dolls and cars in her sandbox. A couple of hours later, she picked up her dollhouse and headed for the side door. She didn't know that her daddy was watching her out of the kitchen window. Just as she reached the porch, her foot caught on a root. Her father watched as if in slow motion a look of horror come over her face. She tumbled down on top of the dollhouse, and it crumbled beneath her eight-year-old weight. His first instinct was to run to her, but he held himself back to watch what she would do.

Looking around quickly, she took the pieces of the house and began to hide them under the porch steps. That night at dinner, nothing was said about the dollhouse. The little girl was quiet and asked to be excused before the meal was finished. By Sunday afternoon, she could take it no longer. She went to the porch steps, gathered the broken pieces in her arms, and with tears streaming down her face, brought them to her father. With tears streaming down his face, the dad took the pieces from her trembling hands and hugged her. He told her she should have obeyed his instructions, but he could fix the dollhouse, and everything was going to be okay.

Why are we so like this little girl? When we make a mess of our lives by disobeying our Father's instructions, we tend to look for solutions anywhere else besides the one who made us and died to redeem us. We try to patch things up with our own childish wisdom, or turn to our favourite addictions to numb the pain of the brokenness. At the heart of all our sinfulness is idolatry: trying to find life, strength, and hope in someone or something other than the source of life. Many competing voices invite us to "come," just as there has been throughout human history.

SPRING OF LIVING WATER

God says to Israel in Jeremiah 2:13: "*My people have committed two sins: They have forsaken me, the spring of living water, and have dug their own cisterns, broken cisterns that cannot hold water.*" All God wanted was for them to trust and obey Him, but they insisted that they were fine on their own. They continually turned to the culture around them for answers. When they needed rain—a vital resource for an agricultural society— they did what their culture did instead of praying to God and trusting that He would be their faithful provider. They began to worship Ba'al and Asherah, the fertility god and goddess of the region. If Israel's God didn't come through, they had to hedge their bets with the fertility god.

They traded faith in Yahweh—the living God of Israel, their spring of living water—for make-believe gods, broken cisterns that couldn't even hold water let alone produce it. We may not worship idols of stone today, but the gods of our culture are no less real!

Who do you put your trust in? When there's more month left at the end of your money and you're unsure where this week's groceries are coming from, do you trust a credit card or do you put your trust in God, your provider? He's your spring of living water!

What do you turn to when things get tough? What takes the edge off? The thrill of a gambling risk? Pornography? Late night pizza? Binge-watching a season on Netflix? A bottle of scotch? Going through your stock portfolio? Maybe you bury yourself in work, or even church meetings. Just push harder; the adrenaline kicks in, and you can keep going a little longer.

I remember getting away for a couple of days on a prayer retreat during a particularly difficult season of ministry. The senior leader of our church had just resigned under a great deal of conflict with the church board, and as the assistant pastor, I was being asked to step into the lead chair for a few months. It was a pressure cooker and had been for months. I arrived at the retreat centre, was led to my room, and began to unpack. I threw some things in a drawer and sat down on the edge of the bed. It felt as though my whole body was vibrating. I'd been going so hard for so long, I didn't realize that I was depending on a constant adrenaline rush to keep going. I remember thinking in that moment: *This can't be the way we're supposed to live*. I was right. Sadly, I've been at that place a few times since then and have had to learn this lesson more than once over the years.

When Jesus says, "Come to me, all you who are weary and burdened," He's saying that people who are stressed, overwhelmed, and weary have all kinds of empty solutions that don't help them. If they'd come to Jesus, they'd find something else. They would be coming to the one who shaped them in their mother's womb, who knows their frame and remembers that they are dust. They would be coming to the one who loved them enough to die in their place to redeem them, restore them, and give them abundant life. They would find hope instead of fear, strength instead of guilt, and life instead of another list of expectations.

What are we waiting for? Bring the burdened-down, broken pieces of your life to the author of life, the architect of your physical, emotional, and spiritual selves, and surrender all you are to Him. He knows what to do. How do you do that? Just like that little girl in our story— with humility, maybe some tears, but certainly by admitting you can't fix it. Call out to your maker, your Heavenly Papa, and ask Him to step in and have His way. Everyone who calls on the name of the Lord will be rescued; they will be saved (Joel 2:32).

Take a moment right now and write down the top three things you tend to turn to instead of Jesus. Confess it as idolatry and ask for forgiveness. Then bring the stuff you've been hiding under the steps to Him and let Him take them this time. It's time to begin a new pattern of finding your hope in Christ.

Questions
FOR REFLECTION AND DISCUSSION

1. What is a prominent memory of an invitation you have accepted or rejected?

2. Have you ever heard/sensed God clearly giving you an invitation to come to Him? How did you respond?

3. What are the top two things you've turned to, instead of God, during times of trouble?

4. What do you think would be different if you turned to God and trusted Him in those situations?

5. What do you need to surrender to God today?

Chapter Three
A PLACE OF REST

"… and I will give you rest."
(Matthew 11:28)

"Men tire themselves in pursuit of rest."
—Laurence Sterne[4]

"You have made us for Yourself and our heart is
restless until it rests in you."
—St. Augustine[5]

"I will give you rest." Do those words stir up longing in your heart? Are you in need of rest? Do you hear Jesus' promises to give you rest and peace and respond with, "Yeah, don't I wish!"?

---

[4] "Laurence Sterne Quotes," AZ Quotes, accessed January 23, 2019, accessed March 4, 2019, https://www.azquotes.com/quote/926194.
[5] Henry Chadwick (trans.), *Confessions* (Oxford: Oxford University Press, 1991), 3.

Jesus' doesn't throw out these words indiscriminately at any passerby, but directs them to people who feel "weary and burdened." He may hope that everyone will be willing to admit their need of His help, but often it's not until we're at a point of desperation that we can see or admit our need.

Just a couple of chapters earlier, Matthew recounts a moment in Jesus' ministry when He was overcome with the emotional, physical, and spiritual needs He saw all around Him: "*When he saw the crowds, he had compassion on them, because they were harassed and helpless, like sheep without a shepherd*" (Matthew 9:36). He saw people wandering aimlessly through life, without purpose, like sheep who'd been left to themselves by careless or absentee shepherds. They'd become lost in a wilderness of their own pain and sinfulness, caught in the thickets with no one to give them hope. All were weary from trying to find their way. All were carrying burdens, and like a traveller who doesn't realize how heavy their backpack is until they take it off, they were oblivious to the crushing weight they carried with them everywhere they went.

THE PROBLEM WITH RELIGION

These people not only were weary of their own lost-ness and the burdens of their own sin, guilt, and shame, but they'd grown up in a religious system that misunderstood the purpose of the Torah, or the Law. As a result, it underestimated the goodness and grace of God and had piled layer upon layer of religious expectation on the shoulders of already broken people, leaving them with no hope whatsoever. Jesus said: "*They* [the teachers of the Law and the Pharisees] *tie up heavy, cumbersome loads and put them on other people's shoulders, but they themselves are not willing to lift a finger to move them*" (Matthew 23:4).

Religious approaches to the laws of God keep us enslaved to our own sin rather than setting us free, because we become obsessed with our brokenness instead of obsessed with the goodness of God. Paul says that this misses the point of the Law: "*Therefore no one will be declared righteous in God's sight by the works of the law; rather, through the law we become conscious of our sin*" (Romans 3:20). No amount of rule-keeping will actually gain us righteous standing in the sight of God. That's not why He gave the Law and not what we should be using it for. The Law is to be a standard to hold up to our lives so that we realize how desperately lost we are and how badly we need a Saviour. We become aware of our sinfulness by the Law.

Religious systems miss this point and try to enforce a level of righteousness through obedience to laws and rules. They not only expect people to keep the laws of scripture, but they add their own. When someone already knows how messed up and broken their lives are, the news that they can put their life back together by simply keeping this long list of rules is not good news. It is, in fact, a harsh burden that will turn them away from the path of faith.

Jesus doesn't snuff out a smoldering wick or break a bruised reed (Matthew 12:20). He realistically assesses the fragility of the worn soul and seeks to lift burdens and heal brokenness wherever He sees it. If Jesus is an exact representation of the Father (Hebrews 1:3), then you can be assured that this is God's attitude toward you today.

Jesus' message was characteristically out of sync with the Jewish religious attitudes of his day. At every turn, the Pharisees (the group most closely aligned with Jesus' teachings—His denomination, you might say) were frustrated with Jesus colouring outside their lines. Early in His ministry, they even plotted to kill Him (Mark 3:6). Jesus' attitude, life, and message were a welcome oasis, an unexpected paradise in the midst of a wasteland of harsh judgement and condemnation, so people flocked to hear Him speak (which also upset the Pharisees). He provided a contrast to the attitudes and behaviour of the religious leaders.

Luke provides an example of the consternation Jesus caused: "*Now the tax collectors and sinners were all drawing near to hear [Jesus]. But the Pharisees and the teachers of the law muttered, 'This man welcomes sinners and eats with them*" (Luke 15:1–2). The teachers of the Law were jealous because they had to guilt and intimidate people to gather a crowd, and here this upstart rabbi had people flocking hillsides, filling beaches, and ripping the roofs off houses to hear Him. *What has He got that we don't?* they wondered.

Jesus invites us into the painful contrast as He tells three stories. In each story we encounter an individual who has lost something: a sheep, a coin, and a son. In each case, when the lost is found, they celebrate extravagantly, because there's nothing like finding what was lost. I can relate to this!

I'm a pen guy. I like pens … what can I say? I don't wear them in a pocket protector or anything, but I'm a pen nerd just the same. I have about five or six pens that I value highly, and when one of them goes missing—as they do from time to time—look out! My family knows to just stay out of the way when Dad is missing a pen. I'll tear furniture apart and dig through everything to find my pen. I'm like a man on a mission, because I won't stop until the pen is found. Until the pen is found, I can't think about anything else. (I'm aware of my need for counselling.) I recently lost one of my pens—a wooden one made by my uncle, who's a pen artisan. (Maybe the pen thing just runs in the family.) I searched everywhere I could think of, but to no avail. It was missing for a couple of months, and I despaired of finding it at all. Every few days I'd search everywhere I'd already looked, as if it would materialize if I looked hard enough. Then one day, my daughter Chelsea moved a small table in a corner of our family room, and there it was. I did a joy dance! It wasn't pretty, but necessary—the lost had been found!

Jesus said this reaction was consistent with the heartbeat of Heaven. When a person is lost, Heaven's efforts are bent on finding that one. No price is too great, even if God Himself has to come down and lay down His own life. He will … He did. When one lost soul returns to its maker, all of Heaven throws an extravagant party and does a joy dance, because the lost has been found.

In the third story, Jesus introduces a contrasting character—the older brother of the lost son. Jesus includes this character as a representative of the religious bunch who don't have the heart of Heaven but miserable, selfish hearts that are more concerned with the rules than the relationship. Is it any wonder the Pharisees and scribes had difficulty drawing crowds of their own?

The religious leaders not only piled a heavy load of rules on the people, but they walked around like morality police, examining people's lives and making sure they were toeing the line. You can understand why Jesus' words "Come to me and I will give you rest" were a welcomed change from "I'm coming after you, so you'd better be good."

RESTORING YOUR SOUL

To whom does Jesus offer His kind of rest? The ones who had tried really hard? The people who had it almost all together but just needed a little break? Yes, but not only them. He offered His rest to Lazarus and his sisters, a family that probably had a bit of money, and also to the wealthy women who funded His ministry. He also cleansed lepers, healed the lame, delivered the demonized, forgave thieves and extortionists, and lifted the eyes of the shame-filled adulteress. All of these people found their heaviness replaced with peace and experienced a return of strength to their lives because they'd found shelter in the love and grace of Jesus.

Psalm 23:1–3a provides perspective on God's desire for us to experience the kind of rest that brings us life:

"*The Lord is my shepherd; I shall not want. He makes me lie down in green pastures. He leads me beside quiet waters. He restores my soul ...*" (NASB). Your Heavenly Father intends for you to enter seasons in which you will lie down and rest, as if in a beautiful meadow. And if He has to, He'll make you rest.

I remember laying down on a hammock in our back yard once during a busy summer. I think it was the first time I'd tried out the hammock, even though we'd had if for a couple of years. I looked above me at the blue sky and saw a cloud that looked incredibly like a man running across the sky. I realized in that moment that it had been years since I'd taken the time to notice the clouds enough to see shapes in them. A silly thing, but it spoke to me profoundly about my lack of making moments of rest in which I could allow the Lord to restore my soul. I spent much more time on the hammock that summer.

Psalm 23 says that God leads us, but He can only lead us if we will follow. If we're truly being led by God, we will, from time to time, walk through the "valley of the shadow of death," but God will also lead us to places of renewal. He will pour in the resources needed for each day, and when we get overwhelmed, He'll wait for us to run to Him so that He can lead us to the meadow. When your soul is utterly depleted and you have nothing left to give, He will—if you allow Him—restore your energy, peace, and joy.

Nothing is more restoring for me than to rest beside natural water—a river, the ocean, the end of a dock on a calm lake. Something elemental touches a deep place in my soul like nothing else can. It seems I'm not the only one to experience this; in fact, I think God created these places with the power to soothe and refresh the human soul. Perhaps He made the human soul with a receptor for whatever these bodies of water give off. Either way, the Father wants to take you to a place "beside quiet waters," where, either literally or metaphorically, you can shut out the distracting noise that has flooded your life with weariness and allow the gentle rhythms of His presence to wash away the clutter. Doesn't seem possible? Carve out a few minutes and the mental space to breathe in the presence of the living God, and He will meet you there.

Why not right now? Why don't you set this book down for a few minutes, find a quiet space, close your eyes, and just be still. Listen … not to the noises around you, but for the whisper of Heaven. Maybe you'll hear nothing, and that's okay. Maybe that's what you need to hear. But maybe you'll sense God's presence surrounding you and bringing you a taste of that peace you long for.

You back? At the end of the psalm, the psalmist says that He will prepare a table for you in the presence of your enemies. Even in the place of greatest conflict, we can find a place of peace. We often think of peace as a lack of conflict, but that's not true peace—it's only a ceasefire. True peace doesn't depend on our external circumstances; rather, it orders our internal world to be secure in God's presence, regardless of our momentary state of affairs. This is the kind of rest and peace Jesus gives when we come to Him. He offers a lasting peace, so we can actually learn to live there. Pursuing the presence of God requires determination and a willingness to come to Him in every situation.

In one of the churches where I served as assistant pastor, I realized there was some serious trouble early in my tenure. Most people in the church weren't aware of the issues, but a contingency of the board and a few they had gathered around them were holding regular secret meetings to figure out how to get rid of the lead pastor. These meetings started when he'd been there less than a year.

Things got very intense and began to affect the health of the senior leader, to the point where he decided to resign for the sake of him and his family. When he left, I became the primary preacher and worship leader for a time. It was one of the most pressure-cooker-like seasons of ministry I've ever experienced. Everything in me wanted to run. I'd get up on Sunday morning, knowing what some of those people had done and said behind closed doors, undermining the pastor and hurting his family, and would have to lead them in worship and preach God's Word to them.

How did I do it? I'd like to tell you that I had such wisdom and leadership prowess that I knew exactly what to do, never questioned my calling there, and singlehandedly brought about sweeping changes in the life of the church. The truth is, I had no idea what I was doing. I cried out to God, and in the midst of intense spiritual and relational conflict, when I didn't know who I could trust or how I was going to survive, Jesus gave me rest and confidence in my soul to navigate, step by tentative step, through the mess.

I took a crash course in coming to Jesus and learned that even when all seems lost, it isn't. I learned that inner peace can empower us to survive a lot of external turmoil. Unfortunately, I've relearned those lessons many times since.

Whether you're coming to Jesus for the first time or the thousandth time, hear His call: "Come to me, and I will give you rest!" Let Him be your go-to, your safe shelter. He will not disappoint.

Questions
FOR REFLECTION AND DISCUSSION

1. Identify one season in your life that was particularly stormy or difficult.

2. How did you respond/deal with the stress of that season?

3. What would you do differently today to bring about a different outcome?

4. What is your favourite quiet place? What about it makes it a place of refuge for you?

5. What would it look like in your daily life and schedule to take a few moments to retreat into the presence of Jesus?

6. How are you letting God train you in retreating to/ living from peace?

Chapter Four
A RELATIONSHIP LIKE NO OTHER

"Take My yoke upon you ..."
(Matthew 11:29)

When the Bible speaks of following Jesus, it is
proclaiming a discipleship which will liberate
mankind from all man-made dogmas, from every
burden and oppression, from every anxiety and
torture which afflicts the conscience. If they
follow Jesus, men escape from the hard yoke of
their own laws, and submit to the kindly
yoke of Jesus Christ.
—Dietrich Bonhoeffer[6]

If there's one phrase in these verses that stands out as
incomprehensible to today's Western church culture,
it would be this one: *"Take my yoke upon you."* It's an

[6] Dietrich Bonhoeffer, *The Cost of Discipleship* (New York: Touchstone, 1959),
37.

outdated, culturally specific religious word picture based on an even older and more outdated farming term. But understanding the phrase is key to understanding what Jesus wanted to communicate to His followers. I need you to dig in with me for a bit and do some hard work with me so that together we can mine the depths of Jesus' words.

Jesus' words are shrouded in the culture of first century rabbinical Judaism. It would be as confusing as if 2,000 years from now someone were to read legal jargon from today's corporate law journals but didn't know enough about the culture or the vocabulary to make sense of it. That's the kind of barrier we need to overcome. If you weren't a part of the Jewish rabbinical culture, you may have missed the implication of His words altogether.

As a young Jewish boy was growing up, he would be expected to begin learning in the local synagogue school around the age of five. He would learn to read and write as well as memorize portions of the Torah (the first five books of the Old Testament, the Law). More dedicated study of the Torah would start around age ten, culminating in his graduation from this portion of his studies at age fourteen. At that point, most boys would leave formal education and begin training with their father in the family business. The brightest students would continue their studies until they were eighteen, training as scribes and teachers of the Law. Those who showed promise of becoming rabbis themselves would then seek out a rabbi from whom they wanted to learn. The rabbis would never seek out students/disciples, as there was a great deal of pride and prestige in being sought out as a rabbi. After rigorous testing, the student (talmid) would be invited to "take my yoke" by that rabbi.

Taking the yoke of a rabbi meant taking the privilege and responsibility of learning his teachings, his way of interpreting scripture, and his way of life. The young talmid was in for a challenging life over the next few years. His rabbi would become his master in all things, and his authority would be greater in the talmid's life than that of his parents or anyone else. The student would be expected to surrender his own will to the will of his master.

A literal yoke is a wooden frame worn by an animal (donkey, horse, ox) or pair of animals in order to harness their strength to accomplish tasks such as plowing a field or pulling a heavy cart. In this case, the will of the animal is bent entirely to the will of the driver. They have to go where the driver wants to go, and they must stop when the driver compels them to do so. Their strength is not their own, but their energy is expended to accomplish the difficult task chosen for them by their master.

In order for the talmid to be conformed to the rabbi in teaching and lifestyle, their will was surrendered and their energy was given to accomplishing the purposes and vision of the rabbi in all things. Only then could they learn to value what the rabbi valued and live the way he lived.

Now let's look at how the process unfolded in the case of Jesus the rabbi. Unlike the proud rabbis of his day, Jesus sought out His disciples. God's activity in our lives is always a product of His love for us, of Him seeking us, not of us seeking Him. We only seek Him because He first sought us. We only love Him because He first loved us!

Jesus came seeking. That's why He left Heaven and was born among a humble class of people—because He was on a mission to seek out the lost sheep. I have a relationship with God and am serving Him as a pastor because He sought me out. I have no idea why! I was a selfish, arrogant guy. I was sarcastic and cynical, and sometimes still am. But Jesus came seeking me and somehow broke through all of my smokescreens and attitude, saying, "I want you!" I don't understand how or why, but I'm glad His love and patience won out!

When Jesus went seeking for disciples, rather than looking among the top ninety-eighth percentile of the graduates of the synagogue schools, He looked for tradesmen. This means that many of His disciples would have bailed on formal education by the age of fourteen. They weren't the ones who showed great aptitude for religious learning. Their families had no illusions of them becoming social, political, or religious leaders of their day. In fact, few could even believe that they would contribute anything to society. They were just average guys.

You don't have to pass an SAT test to become His disciple. He isn't looking for the over-achiever, or the person who has their life all together. In fact, when Jesus got grief from other rabbis about the company He was keeping, He said, "*It is not the healthy who need a doctor, but the sick. But go and learn what this means: 'I desire mercy, not sacrifice.' For I have not come to call the righteous, but sinners"* (Matthew 9:12–13).

In Matthew 11:28, Jesus throws His invitation so wide, it could blow the mind of every first century rabbi … and it should ours as well! He invites everyone who is weary and heavy burdened to come and take His yoke, to be His rabbinical disciple.

Jesus elevated the value of every person. He valued women above the status given them by His culture; He valued Gentiles above the status given them by other Jewish teachers; He valued the poor, the lepers, the sinful, children, and so on. He also holds you in high value. He died for you and rose for you. He gave everything to redeem you, and He wants you to receive all the benefits of being a disciple, a learner, of Him.

To become a disciple of Christ, we must take on His yoke and surrender our stubborn will to His. To taste of the benefits of His mastery in our circumstances, we must accept His mastery of our lives. We cannot enjoy the benefits of the Christ-life without the commitment to live the Christ-life. There's no such thing as an un-surrendered follower of Jesus Christ. That's what Dietrich Bonhoeffer called "cheap grace" in his great book, *The Cost of Discipleship*:

> Costly grace confronts us as a gracious call to follow Jesus, it comes as a word of forgiveness to the broken spirit and the contrite heart. It is costly because it compels a man to submit to the yoke

of Christ and follow him; it is grace because Jesus says: "My yoke is easy and my burden is light."[7]

We cannot have the benefit of God's grace and remain masters of our own destiny.

Jesus said that if we love Him, we will keep His commands, but those commands are not burdensome (1 John 5:3). Jesus' commands are to love. Period.

In Matthew 22:37–40, Jesus sums up all the commands of the Jewish scriptures, our Old Testament, with these words:

> "Love the Lord your God with all your heart and with all your soul and with all your mind." This is the first and greatest commandment. And the second is like it: "Love your neighbor as yourself." All the Law and the Prophets hang on these two commandments.

Jesus' message of love was quite different from what other teachers said about the Jewish scriptures.

On the night before Jesus went to the cross, He gave one more commandment: "A new command I give you: Love one another. As I have loved you, so you must love one another. By this everyone will know that you are my disciples, if you love one another" (John 13:34–35). Along with loving God and our neighbour, we are to love one another as believers with the kind of love that Jesus showed us—the kind of love in which we lay down our lives for others. This kind of love distinguishes His followers from everyone else in

---

[7] Ibid., 45.

the world. That is the extent of His commands. That is His yoke.

I know that may sound easier than it is. Loving God and others can be a real challenge sometimes, especially when we're so bent on loving ourselves more. But obeying these commandments is its own reward. To love and enjoy the richness of connectedness that comes from obeying that command will fill your life with a blessing and fulfillment that all the duty-bound commands in the world can't give.

The path of love is one that will exact much from you. It's not an easy path, and at every turn it will ask you to put someone else ahead of your own comfort. That's the definition of God-style love. It means deciding to walk the path of love, even when it costs you something. That's what Jesus did, and that's what He calls us to do.

Jesus wants to be your rabbi. He wants to teach you how to interpret scripture and how to love God and others as you walk this journey of life. If you haven't already, won't you consider taking the yoke of Jesus? Won't you surrender your life to Him? You won't be the loser in the deal! You'll learn how to deal with your circumstances with strength and grace, how to love the people around you better, and how to trust your Heavenly Father as Jesus did when He walked on the earth.

There may be someone reading this book who is a not-yet-convinced seeker of truth, or who has faith in Christ but has given up on trying to be part of a church. (Thanks for making it this far.) You might be saying something like, "Wait a minute! My encounters with church have been anything but what you're describing! They didn't make burdens lighter; they were miserable people who weren't happy until other people were miserable too."

Let me first say that I feel your pain. The church hasn't always done well understanding or representing the message of the freedom and life Jesus came to bring. I've been both a victim and a perpetrator of that reality. Even though the church is called to reflect Christ to the world, we shouldn't imagine her failures as a part of that reflection.

Also, not every church is like that. There are some terrific churches out there, where people learn to bear the yoke of Christ. They learn to love well (albeit imperfectly) their Lord, their neighbours (the world in need), and their brothers and sisters. I'm part of one such community, and they are a joy to be around.

There's no relationship like the one we have with Christ as His disciples. He invites us to know Him, love Him, and serve Him unreservedly, and He provides us with everything we need to do it. He simply wants to delight in the partnership that comes from working in us, with us, and through us.

"Jesus asks nothing of us without giving us the strength to perform it. His commandment never seeks to destroy life, but to foster, strengthen and heal it."[8]

---

[8] Ibid., 38.

Questions
FOR REFLECTION AND DISCUSSION

1. When did you begin your relationship with Jesus? What circumstances led you to turn to Him?

2. What makes your relationship with Him similar to other relationships? What makes it different?

3. Does the command to love feel heavy to you? Why?

4. How do you think Jesus wants to give you the ability to love when it's difficult to do?

5. In what ways do you need to choose today to take up Jesus' yoke? What areas of your life have not yet come under His Lordship and mastery?

Chapter Five
LEARNING FROM THE MASTER
—A SUSTAINABLE LIFE

*"... and learn from me, for I am gentle
and humble in heart ..."*
(Matthew 11:29)

"There is not in the world a kind of life more
sweet and delightful than that of a continual
conversation with God."
—Brother Lawrence[9]

This was always the part of this passage that I couldn't understand. One of the reasons for this was Mr. Jackson. Mr. Jackson was my sixth-grade teacher. He was a stark contrast from my fifth-grade teacher, Mr. Neil, and my seventh-grade teacher, Mr. Poortinga. Mr. Jackson was the coolest teacher I had in elementary school. He was laid

---

[9] Brother Lawrence, *The Practice of the Presence of God,* accessed March 4, 2019, https://www.ccel.org/ccel/lawrence/practice.pdf.

back about classroom discipline and tried to be friends with all of the students. He was a really nice guy, but I learned very little in his class.

Mr. Neil and Mr. Poortinga, on the other hand, were both principals and teachers. They were strict disciplinarians and no-nonsense kind of guys. You knew they cared, but you also knew there were boundaries not to be crossed. I learned a lot from them because they expected more from me and believed there was more for me.

Whenever I'd read about Jesus as gentle and humble of heart, I always pictured Mr. Jackson. I always thought Jesus was talking about His teaching methods. In other words, "Learn from me, because I will take it really easy on you. I won't expect too much, so you can just chill in my class, learn at your own pace, and we'll have a great time!" I'm not sure how well I'd learn from that Jesus. I'd probably try and get away with as little work as I could. I know you're not all that different from me. You probably wouldn't learn much either.

But what if Jesus wasn't describing his teaching methods? I've come to believe He was talking about His living methods. Rather than receiving academic instruction from Him, we're meant to follow His way of life. If we can learn to be like Him in our attitude, we'll find the path of peace and rest in the same way He does.

When Jesus said He was gentle and humble of heart, I believe He meant that He never seeks His own agenda or way, but in everything listens to His Father and follows His lead. Jesus indicates that doing life this way removes huge amounts of fear and stress, and things tend to work out well a lot more often.

DO WHAT HE SEES HIM DO

In John 5:19–21, Jesus describes the first aspect of this kind of life:

> *So Jesus said to them, "Truly, truly, I say to you, the Son can do nothing of his own accord, but only what he sees the Father doing. For whatever the Father does, that the Son does likewise. For the Father loves the Son and shows him all that he himself is doing. And greater works than these will he show him, so that you may marvel. For as the Father raises the dead and gives them life, so also the Son gives life to whom he will."* (ESV)

The most shocking phrase in this passage is "… *the Son can do nothing* …". Umm, what? This is the Son of God we're talking about, the second person of the Trinity. By Him, and for Him, the universe was created … and He could do nothing?

To understand this, we need to understand an important theological truth found in Philippians 2. Theologians call this the "kenosis," or the emptying. The Son of God, when He chose to enter into human history and become our Saviour, emptied Himself of supernatural power and glory. He laid aside anything that would make Him more than human in order to take on human flesh and truly be one of us. Anything less would be cheating!

Jesus chose to limit Himself to living in utter dependence on His Father and by the power of the Holy Spirit in order to accomplish His mighty works on planet Earth.

Jesus didn't just walk around Galilee and Judea looking to see what trouble He could stir up … He actually lived every day in humble dependence on His Father. When He saw that the Father's desire was to heal, He would reach out His hand and heal. When He saw that His Father was broken-hearted over someone's pain, He would encourage them. When He saw that His Father's desire was to respond to a grieving widow by bringing her son back to life, He would do the culturally unthinkable and not only interrupt the funeral procession, but touch the casket (even more scandalous) and ruin the funeral by raising the boy from the dead.

This humble submission to His Father was an incredible way to live and minister. It took the pressure off! It wasn't Jesus' responsibility to "perform" for anyone. He wasn't responsible to produce results—He just did what He knew His Father would bless and trusted the results to Him. Because Jesus was completely connected to His Father, He always got results.

Jesus was never flustered by the expectations of others, because His only desire was to follow His Father's lead and bring joy to Him. When Peter came to Jesus and warned Him that everyone was looking for Him, Jesus replied: "*Let us go somewhere else—to the nearby villages—so I can preach there also. That is why I have come*" (Mark 1:38). He was unmoved by the expectations of people and remained totally committed to the pleasure of His Father.

How much of our anxiety comes from taking on the demands and expectations of others? If you're like me, the majority of your stress is borrowed from someone else! I received a letter once from someone I cared for very much, and they made it clear that they weren't happy with some decisions I had made. Because of unhealthy emotional boundaries (or lack thereof) in our relationship, I'd given them enough room in my life that I allowed their opinion to shape my emotional well-being. They were upset with me, and I accepted their expectations as my own, spinning my world into emotional turmoil. I turned to a pastor friend who helped me construct healthy boundaries around my life. I could then see that there was no reason to feel the weight of the other party's expectations. Pam and I had prayerfully weighed our options and knew we were doing the best thing for our family. I didn't need to borrow stress from this other person. It was their baggage to deal with. That was a very freeing moment, because we knew who we were and whose we were.

At His baptism, and also on the Mount of Transfiguration, Jesus heard the love and approval of His Heavenly Father. No other voice mattered after that. No one's fear caused Jesus to become anxious, no one's anger caused Him to be insecure, no one's disappointment caused Him to try to perform for their approval. Life was much less complicated for Him because He simply lived, moment by moment, to do what His Father asked

Him to do. He lived in humble dependence on God and, therefore, in peace in every situation.

SPEAK WHAT HE HEARS HIM SAY

I've met a lot of people who said they spoke for God, and some of them really did. They couldn't possibly have known the things they knew unless God had whispered into their hearts by His Spirit. God often uses a friend of mine to give words of knowledge. He has spoken things so personal and specific that they caused the other person to literally fall to their knees in awe of God's power and in repentance.

I have also known people who claimed to speak the words of God, but the poison in their words actually belied the venom of bitterness in their own soul. Their harsh and controlling attitude revealed that they were grasping for control of their own crippling fears. Their words and the spirit in which they were spoken did not reflect God's character. Jesus' ears were tuned to hear the Father's words. He never presumed to speak in His own authority, but only what He heard the Father say:

> *When you have lifted up the Son of Man, then you will know that I am he and that I do nothing on my own but speak just what the Father has taught me. The one who sent me is with me; he has not left me alone, for I always do what pleases him.* (John 8:28–29)

Jesus did nothing on His own authority but spoke the words His Father gave Him to speak. How did the pre-adolescent Jesus wow the teachers of the Law with His wisdom and understanding? He was already skilled at hearing what the Father was saying.

The first recorded time Jesus taught in public, people were *"amazed at his teaching, because he taught as one who had authority, and not as their teachers of the law"* (Matthew 7:28–29). Every time Jesus opened His mouth to teach, brilliant wisdom—the likes of which the world had never heard—came out. The Father shaped the human heart and knows how we think and how life should work. As He spoke the wisdom of the ages to His Son, the Son spoke it to us. When asked difficult questions, He didn't panic or clam up. He listened, and time after time left His opponents tripping over their own foolishness.

Jesus not only taught us the wisdom and ways of God, but how to access them ourselves.

What would change in your relationships, workplace, or ministry opportunities if, rather than speak the first thing that comes to mind in a given situation, you stopped for a moment and listened to the voice of God by His Holy Spirit? Jesus explained that He intended to give us answers we'd never studied for and words that came from a source beyond our own minds:

> *On my account you will be brought before governors and kings as witnesses to them and to the Gentiles. But when they arrest you, do not worry about what*

to say or how to say it. At that time you will be given what to say, for it will not be you speaking, but the Spirit of your Father speaking through you. (Matthew 10:18–20)

Jesus didn't intend for persecution to be the only instance in which we'd have access to such sources of supernatural wisdom; He was assuring His disciples that even in moments like that, they could trust that the power that was available to them every day would not abandon them. The gifts of the Spirit, such as words of wisdom/knowledge, aren't spooky, mysterious things, like in *Invasion of the Body Snatchers*, where something takes control of you. They're simply moments when you listen, and the Spirit of God gives you what you need for the moment.

WHEN BRANCHES TRY TO BE VINES

Jesus is always with us, as He promised, and always ready to supply what we lack. Paul says that he will boast about his weaknesses, because they give opportunity for the glory and power of Christ to be displayed in his life. When we are weak, then we are strong (2 Corinthians 12:10).

Trouble comes when we think we can supply all our needs. This was Adam and Eve's original sin, and we still fall prey to its temptation today. Eve thought God was holding out on her, and that she and Adam could find a path to greater wisdom and power apart from God. She disconnected from her dependency on God and made the choice to be her own source of strength. God didn't make her to be a vine ... He made her to be a branch. She was never supposed to become disconnected from God's unending supply of life and strength and wisdom. When she and Adam chose to do that, they unplugged all of us from this amazing way of life for which we were made. That's what Paul means when he says that we were dead in our transgressions and sins (Ephesians 2:1).

Jesus came to reconcile us to the Father and reconnect us in a dependent relationship:

> *I am the true vine, and my Father is the gardener. He cuts off every branch in me that bears no fruit, while every branch that does bear fruit he prunes so that it will be even more fruitful. You are already clean because of the word I have spoken to you. Remain in me, as I also remain in you. No branch can bear fruit by itself; it must remain in the vine. Neither can you bear fruit unless you remain in me. I am the vine; you are the branches. If you remain in me and I in you, you will bear much fruit; apart from me you can do nothing. If you do not remain in me, you are like a branch that is thrown away and withers; such branches are picked up, thrown into the fire and burned. If you remain in me and my words remain in you, ask whatever you wish, and it will be done for you. This is to my Father's glory, that you bear much fruit, showing yourselves to be my disciples.* (John 15:1–8)

Jesus connects the dots for us and shows us that the relationship He had with His Father on Earth is the kind of relationship we can have with Him. Just as He could do nothing without the Father, we can do nothing without Him. In the same way He had the life and power of Heaven flowing through Him, we can have the life and power of Jesus flowing through us when we walk in intimacy with Him. We're called to learn from Him and live like Him, for He is gentle and lowly of heart.

Jesus invites us to remain/abide in Him, promising that He will remain/abide in us. This abiding—staying connected in a life-giving relationship to our source—is the key to fruitful ministry. It requires of us a continual awareness of the presence of Jesus in our lives, and an ongoing surrender to His will. This doesn't happen by accident but by turning our hearts to Him moment by moment. In some seasons this requires more discipline than others.

In seasons that require more focused attention on abiding, my wife and I set an alarm on our phone that goes off every few minutes. Every time it does, we're reminded to turn our hearts again to the presence of Jesus. This creates an ongoing conversation and connection with Him that keeps the heart anchored.

After stating that He is the true vine, His Father the vine dresser, and we the branches, Jesus again states: "*I am the vine; you are the branches*" (John 15:5). He knows we get this confused *way* too easily. It's like He's saying, "Listen up, guys. Don't forget who you are, and don't forget whose strength is going to get things done!"

Much of the fear, anxiety, and stress we carry in life comes from getting this relationship mixed up. When things seem to go wrong and we believe we have to resolve the situation with our own resources, we carry a weight we were never intended to carry. When your friend or child wanders from God, and you believe it's your job to bring them back, you take on your shoulders the work of the Holy Spirit. When someone needs a miracle and you pray harder, trying to find the right (magic) words to pray, you're taking on the role of the vine. When you get hit with a financial blow and are thrown into a tailspin of fear, you're trying to be the provider rather than trusting the one who is.

When we mix up this relationship, we live in overwhelming anxiety that can never produce results. There is another way: the way of the bottomless cup. In this way, we understand that we're only the jar of clay. If we trust Jesus and live every moment in dependence on Him, He will show His all-surpassing glory through us (see 2 Corinthians 4:7). When we are weak, then we are strong.

INTIMACY IS THE KEY

To access this life, Jesus listened moment by moment to the voice of His Father and kept the Father's activity in the centre of His vision. For us, it means abiding/remaining in the presence of Jesus, listening for His voice and being aware of His activity.

My dad was a welder, a millwright, a backyard mechanic, and, in his later years, an electrician and cabinetmaker. He could fix anything that was fixable, whether it was metal, electrical, mechanical, wood, or any combination thereof! From my earliest days, I would hold a light for him and pass him the tools he asked for. I was his little helper. I remember being six years old and holding a light while he fixed the car in the dark. Never get a six-year-old to hold a light when you're trying to see what you're doing! There are too many cool things to look at in an engine to focus on just one spot! When I was a teenager and he had his own business, I worked for him in the summer, fixing farm equipment and doing contract work for factories.

By the time I was twenty, I knew what he needed even before he spoke a word. We knew each other so well, we could read each other's non-verbal communications. He often wanted me on the job just because we could work like a team better than anyone else in the company. Our intimacy enabled me to know what no one else could know and follow what no one else could follow. Jesus wants to have that and more with us. He wants us to feel His compassion for people, to anticipate what He would do when we see someone hurting, to be right where He would be when our co-worker or neighbour goes through a tragedy.

KNOWING HIM

Peter draws a significant connection between our intimacy with God and His glory and power flowing through our lives.

> *His divine power has given us everything we need for a godly life through our knowledge of him who called*

us by his own glory and goodness. Through these he has given us his very great and precious promises, so that through them you may participate in the divine nature, having escaped the corruption in the world caused by evil desires. (2 Peter 1:3–4)

We don't need to plead with God for the resources necessary to live for Him in this world, as His power supplies everything we need. That sounds like a bottomless cup to me! When you need wisdom, it has been given to you. When you need perseverance, it has been given to you. When you need faith, it has been given to you—not in just enough measure, but it's everything you need. It has been given through our knowledge of Him, so we can't claim these things as ours if we don't know Him. We can't assume that God has our backs if He doesn't have our hearts. Intimacy with Him is essential for tapping into the resources He has made available to us in the cross and by His Spirit.

On the other hand, if we do know Him and are walking with Him in intimacy, we can trust that these resources are ours. Peter says that it's by His great and precious promises that we can actually participate in the divine nature. That almost sounds blasphemous, yet it's God's Word! When we walk with God in friendship and know His heart, He allows us to do God-like things with God-like authority to accomplish His purposes on the Earth.

In Ephesians 1, Paul outlines many of the spiritual blessings that are ours in Christ. Because we're in Christ and our lives are hidden in Him (Colossians 3:3), because we are seated with Him in heavenly realms (Ephesians 2:6), and because God, who did not withhold his own Son, now along with Him will give us all things (Romans 8:32), we have been given many spiritual blessings. These blessings include every spiritual resource we need to do the things God has called us to do. He has our back, but we need to know what God has called us to do. That comes with intimacy.

In Ephesians 1:15–23, Paul prays for the Ephesian church, and presumably for all believers. He prays that God would give us a Spirit of revelation and wisdom so we may know Him better. What's really important? Knowing God! And what else after that?

> … *that you may know the hope to which he has called you, the riches of his glorious inheritance in his holy people, and his incomparably great power for us who believe. That power is the same as the mighty strength he exerted when he raised Christ from the dead and seated him at his right hand in the heavenly realms* … (Ephesians 1:18–20)

We need to know God, but we also need to know the huge resources He has made ours because of the inheritance we have in Christ. When we step out in faith to do the works that Heaven has instructed us to do, we can be confident that all of Heaven will stand behind us!

Jesus' intimacy with His Father enabled Him to function in a daily relationship of trust, as he knew what His Father wanted and could step out in authority to do it. Because He maintained an unceasing flow of intimate communication with the Father, He was able to walk in lockstep with the Father's wishes. This is the key to our authority as well.

HEARING HIM

We not only need to know Jesus to do His works in His power, but we need to be able to hear His voice. I know for some that sounds odd or spooky, and I'm not really talking about an audible voice, although there is biblical precedence for that as well. Jesus speaks to us in many ways and wants us to be people who are guided by His "voice" so that we can be effective for Him.

In 2002, I was driving a U-Haul moving truck filled with all of our earthly possessions. My wife was following in our family vehicle. We were on our way to a new position as a youth and worship pastor and excited about the days ahead. On our way there, we passed through a small town. As the rented truck lumbered through the main street, I heard a whisper in my heart: "You will pastor this town." It startled me, because I was on my way to another place to pastor, but I tucked it away and kept driving.

Five years later when I felt the Lord getting me ready to step out and take on my first lead pastor position, I learned that the pastor in that small town had just resigned. I heard that whisper in my soul again: "You are going to pastor that town." I mentioned this to one of our district leaders, and he brushed me off.

"No," he said, "they're looking for a more seasoned pastor there."

I tucked it away again and kept trusting the Lord to lead us. Three months later, I got a call one evening from the church in that town, asking me if I'd come for an interview. I didn't sleep all night. The Holy Spirit had spoken clearly to me not once, but twice, and I knew He was leading our lives. Sure enough, a few weeks later I was voted in as pastor of that church.

In Acts 16:6–10, Luke writes of Paul and his companions travelling from place to place with the good news of Jesus. But when they tried to enter the Roman province of Asia (the west end of modern Turkey), the Holy Spirit kept them from preaching there. They tried to go into another area, but *the Spirit of Jesus would not allow them to* (Acts 16:7). Hearing the leading of Jesus through His Spirit is key to doing God's work in His way. Little did Paul know that a couple of years later, he would go to Asia, and one of the greatest waves of God's power in all of history would sweep that province. Despite Paul's best intentions to do the work of God, he didn't know the intentions of Jesus. He needed to learn to listen to His voice so that the God-ordained appointments would accomplish His great purposes. Paul may never have gone to Macedonia if he hadn't listened to the Spirit-dream he received. Had he not, the great churches of Philippi and Thessalonica would never have been started.

Just as Jesus listened to the words of His Father, we, the branches, need to listen to the vine. We need Him to lead and guide us. At different times in my life I've followed what I understood to be the voice of Jesus, but it led me in directions that didn't always make sense; however, those moments shaped who I've become and what I've been able to do for God. At other times I wasn't sure I heard correctly, or I chose to do my own thing. It's a process to learn to hear and obey The Voice.

The voice of God can be audible, but often it's a sense of knowing in your spirit that the Holy Spirit is speaking to you at a level deeper than your five senses. Sometimes it's a picture in your mind, or a thought that seems to come from nowhere. Sometimes it's a sense of peace that surrounds a particular decision. It's not the same for every situation or for every person. That's why it's a process of learning to hear.

If you didn't know me and I were to call you out of the blue, you'd have no way of recognizing my voice. But if you and I developed a friendship, and I called you every couple of weeks to chat on the phone, eventually you'd recognize my voice right away. Jesus said:

The one who enters by the gate is the shepherd of the sheep. The gatekeeper opens the gate for him, and the sheep listen to his voice. He calls his own sheep by name and leads them out. When he has brought out all his own, he goes on ahead of them, and his sheep follow him because they know his voice. But they will never follow a stranger; in fact, they will run away from him because they do not recognize a stranger's voice. (John 10:2–5)

Sheep may not have a reputation for being the brightest animals on the planet. In fact, science tells us that the domestication of the sheep reduces their brain size in comparison to undomesticated sheep by almost 25 per cent. This makes me wonder why God compares His people to sheep throughout the pages of scripture! Sheep aren't stupid, however, when it comes to their loyalties. They learn, through the gentle and loving care of their shepherd, to identify his unique voice patterns and can tell the difference between their shepherd and another shepherd or a complete stranger.

The story is told of an American tourist who was travelling in the Middle East. He came upon several shepherds whose flocks had gathered together around a large watering hole. After an exchange of greetings, one of the shepherds turned toward the sheep and called out, "Manah. Manah. Manah." (Manah means "follow me" in Arabic.) Immediately his sheep separated themselves from the rest and followed him.

Then one of the two remaining shepherds called out "Manah, Manah," and his sheep left the common flock to follow him. The traveller said to the third shepherd: "I would like to try that. Let me put on your cloak and turban and see if I can get the rest of the sheep to follow me."

The shepherd smiled knowingly as the traveller wrapped himself in the cloak, put the turban on his head, and called out, "Manah, Manah." The sheep didn't respond to the stranger's voice. Not one of them moved toward him.

Jesus wants not only our belief in Him, but our loyalty. He wants us to care enough to take the time to learn to discern His voice amongst all the clamouring voices of our culture. We are inundated with news bytes, tweets, blogs, advertising media, movie trailers, and catchy songs on the radio. Hundreds of voices scream at you in a day, and all of them want your loyalty. They want you to believe in their message, follow their advice, and buy what they're selling. Add to that the voices in your own mind: the voice of your own opinion, which may or may not line up with God's will and His Word; the voice of your conscience; and the voice of sinful desires that battle for your attention. All of these things present a loud clamour of noise that can make it very difficult to hear clearly what our Shepherd is trying to say. A true disciple, one who wants to take on the yoke of his master, will learn to filter out undeserved and undesired voices. He will do whatever he can to learn to tune in to the frequency of the Master's voice and hear what He's saying.

Learning to hear the Shepherd's voice means spending focused, intentional time reading the Bible. As Christians, we believe the Bible is the Word of God and one of the most important ways God speaks to us. It reveals the character of God and helps us measure the other voices we hear. If they speak contrary in content or attitude to what we see revealed in scripture, we know that they're a counterfeit voice and not the voice of our Shepherd.

The New Testament reveals God in the person of Jesus Christ. He is the *"radiance of God's glory and the exact representation of His being*" (Hebrews 1:3). Our best view of God is through the character of Jesus. If what we hear is contrary to Jesus' priorities or character, then we need to reject it as not from God. Being diligent students of God's Word and His revelation of Himself will align us with the voice of God and help us get on His frequency.

We should expect to hear the voice of the Holy Spirit speaking to us as well. The Spirit will sound like Jesus and the Father, because they are perfectly aligned in their will and ways. The Spirit will speak to you about the big and little things of life. He may prompt you to say hi to someone that He wants you to reach for Jesus, or He may tell you to give generously to someone in need. He may warn you not to invest in a business venture, or tell you to call someone you haven't thought of in years.

Jesus said to Nicodemus: "*The wind blows wherever it pleases. You hear its sound, but you cannot tell where it comes from or where it is going. So it is with everyone born of the Spirit*" (John 3:8). Notice He doesn't say, "So it is with the Spirit," which you might expect Him to say, meaning the Holy Spirit is unpredictable. Rather He says that those who are born of the Spirit will live unpredictable lives, carried along by the leading of the Spirit. There was no adventure like Jesus daily surrendering to the voice of the Father, and there's no adventure today like the followers of Christ daily surrendering to the voice of the Spirit of God.

OBEYING/FOLLOWING HIM

Just as Jesus said and did what He saw the Father doing, we need to not only hear Jesus, our Shepherd's, voice, but do what He says. We need to follow in His footsteps: 1 John 2:6 says, *"whoever says he abides in him ought to walk in the same way in which he walked"* (ESV). In James 1:22, we're told not to just listen to the Word, and so deceive ourselves, but to do what it says. It's actually deadlier to hear Jesus' words, acknowledge their truth, and then fail to live them out than if we'd never heard them at all.

This path of discipleship, this journey of following Jesus, is meant to be a mirror of Jesus' path when following His Father. Jesus expressed this truth to Philip when Philip insisted Jesus tell them the way to the eternal realms of His Father. Jesus said, *"I am the way and the truth and the life"* (John 14:6). When Jesus said to learn from Him because He is gentle and humble of heart, He meant that we were to follow Him in the same way that He followed His Father. This is the way to effective, productive, life-giving ministry: walking in humble obedience to Jesus, following the wind of His presence, doing exactly what He says to do, and going where He says to go. This way of living will impact lives and transform communities, and your own soul will be strengthened and renewed with a sense of mission!

Tucked away in one of the books of the minor prophets in the Old Testament is a picture of the bottomless cup life that was meant to encourage an overwhelmed team of leaders overseeing the rebuilding of the temple in Jerusalem after the return from exile in Babylon (Zechariah 4). They were being opposed by people who didn't want the worship of God restored in Jerusalem. The leaders were wearied by the sheer size of the task and the list of resources that had to be procured to see this nearly-impossible feat accomplished. They knew they didn't have the personal strength or resources to see this dream come to pass, but it was key to the re-establishment of their nation and the purposes of God.

As a pastor, I've overseen more than one building program. At one church, we sold our old building and built a whole new facility on a large piece of property. It was a massive undertaking, and being young and excited about it, I threw myself into it far more than I should have or was necessary. We'd hired an excellent project manager who did a phenomenal job, but I was a part of all major decisions. As exciting as it was, it almost killed me. I had a young family while at the same time leading the church and caring for the spiritual needs of a couple of hundred people. Before the project was done, I was on blood pressure medication and had to wear a heart monitor for a twenty-four-hour period after an episode of arrhythmia. By the time the project was finished, I thought a two-week vacation would get me all rested up, and I'd be back to 100 per cent in no time. On the contrary, it took nearly two years to fully recover physically and emotionally from the toll the project took on me and my leadership.

I learned a great number of lessons through my experience, not least of all that a major building project is incredibly overwhelming for the one leading the charge. This was the position of a man named Zerubbabel.

In Zechariah 4, God sends a message of encouragement to Zerubbabel through the prophet in the form of a picture:

Then the angel who talked with me returned and woke me up, like someone awakened from sleep. He asked me, "What do you see?" I answered, "I see a solid gold lampstand with a bowl at the top and seven lamps on it, with seven channels to the lamps. Also there are two olive trees by it, one on the right of the bowl and the other on its left." I asked the angel who talked with me, "What are these, my lord?" (Zechariah 4:1–4)

The Two Witnesses

God tells Zerubbabel, who is overwhelmed by a big job, that if he walks in trust and obedience, He will keep him connected to a never-ending source of fuel for the job he has to do. In this same passage, we find these well-known words: *"'Not by might nor by power, but by my Spirit,' says the Lord Almighty"* (Zechariah 4:6).

Jesus invites us to come and learn a different way of working, of moving through life, and of serving God. He invites us to learn from Him a rhythm that won't wear us out, a way of approaching life and Christian service in which we can be continually filled with all the strength, love, wisdom, and power to do the things God has called us to do. If we're burning out, we're either doing things God hasn't called us to do, or we're doing them in ways He never intended.

Questions

FOR REFLECTION AND DISCUSSION

1. What do you think about Jesus' statement that He could do nothing by Himself?

2. How does it make you feel about your own life, or your attempts to serve Him?

3. Describe a time you felt overwhelmed by a responsibility or job you had to do.

4. How have you found strength in those moments?

5. What do you think it looks like for you to abide, or stay, in the presence of Jesus? What may need to change in your weekly routines to achieve this?

6. What might you dare to do for Jesus if you had unlimited strength or resources?

Chapter Six
A DEEPER REST—A PLACE TO LIVE

"… and you will find rest for your souls."
(Matthew 11:29)

"Abiding does not mean sitting idly by. It means
resting in the work, resting in the moment,
resting in the truth, resting in the confidence
that God is your provision"
—Robin Bertram[10]

Jesus refers to two types of rest in Matthew 11. The first one is a gift of grace: *"Come to me … and I will give you rest"* (v. 28). He gives to those who are weary and heavy burdened; however, He also says, *"learn from me … and you will find rest for your souls"* (v. 29). We'll experience the second kind of rest when we start to do life in the way of the Master—the way of dependent trust in His presence and power—instead of trying to be self-reliant.

---

[10] Robin Bertram, *No Regrets* (Lake Mary, FL: Charisma House, 2017), 19.

In Chapters Two and Three we unpacked the first type of rest. We find Jesus sending out an invitation to the weary, the burdened, and the broken to come to Him and find a respite from the exhaustion of life. In Jesus we find a place of safety, of renewal. He, our Shepherd, makes us lie down in green pastures and leads us beside quiet waters to restore our souls. I'm so glad for this aspect of Jesus' invitation and for His care of those He loves. I'm also glad that He doesn't want to just be our panic button but to train and equip us to live life differently so that we don't end up there again … or at least not as often!

In this chapter, we'll explore this other kind of rest. It's not a case of unplugging or ceasing activity, but rather doing things in a sustainable way and with a bottomless cup of strength, energy, and passion. This is the treasure in the field I spoke of in the Introduction. If we could get a hold of this, our families would be less chaotic, our churches would be healthier, and fewer of us would experience burnout trying to do the good work God has called us to do.

I can picture God looking down upon all of our efforts to do stuff for Him, and the self-destructive ways in which we try to do it, and saying, "Hey, kids! You're missing something really important! I showed you how to do this stuff, and you're doing it your own way instead. Stop! You're going to hurt yourself or someone else!"

My son is thirteen right now and 6'2". Yes, you read that right. He's fairly strong for his age and is testing out his strength. When the car needs to be moved in the driveway, he actually wants me to put it in neutral so he can push it. That works okay in the driveway, but not so well on the freeway. Many of us do life in a manner akin to putting a car in neutral and convincing a few friends to push us around town in it. (That is, if we have enough friends who like us that much.) The work gets done, but our friends are exhausted and somewhat resentful, and we didn't reach our destination on time because they pushed too slow. Car manufacturers put an engine in the vehicle for a reason: it's the best way to propel the vehicle at the desired speed and for the desired duration without wearing anyone out.

This type of rest encompasses a number of aspects. The first is the principle of "sabbath rest," a rhythm of life that God outlines in scripture. The second is what scripture calls "Promised Land rest," or entering into a new place of living where all is provided for you as you place your confidence in the Provider and not in yourself. These two principles work together to produce a peace-oriented life that always has enough. But let's not get ahead of ourselves.

Studies conducted over the past fifty years reveal that mental health issues are on the increase in North America. A *Psychology Today* blog states that the most marked increase in mental health issues was noted between 1930 and 1990, but it has continued to increase since then. One of the more troubling trends has been mental health issues among children and teens, which has seen a significant increase since the 1990s.[11]

---

[11] Jean M. Twenge, "Are Mental Health Issues on the Rise?" *Psychology Today*, October 12, 2015, accessed on March 4, 2019, https://www.psychologytoday.com/blog/our-changing-culture/201510/are-mental-health-issues-the-rise.

There could be a number of reasons for this trend, but I'd suggest that one contributing factor is the loss of "down time." If we fill every moment of our lives with busyness, whether it be work, school, or even socializing, our minds and bodies never have a chance to reset.

The Rhythm of Sabbath Rest

What do you know about the Sabbath? For the Hebrew people, it was the seventh day of the week—our Saturday. God made a commandment about it … one of the Big Ten:

> *Remember the Sabbath day by keeping it holy. Six days you shall labor and do all your work, but the seventh day is a sabbath to the Lord your God. On it you shall not do any work, neither you, nor your son or daughter, nor your male or female servant, nor your animals, nor any foreigner residing in your towns. For in six days the Lord made the heavens and the earth, the sea, and all that is in them, but he rested on the seventh day. Therefore the Lord blessed the Sabbath day and made it holy.* (Exodus 20:8–11)

For many of us, this is all we know about the sabbath principle. It's a religious restriction on our activity one day a week, but because we've packed our lives so full of stuff to do, it doesn't seem realistic anymore. We downgrade this major commandment to a ridiculous suggestion and just keep going. But we ignore the principle of sabbath to our great peril.

We aren't made for full-on, 24/7 busy lifestyles. God instituted the Sabbath to help us understand that we need a rhythm of work and rest in our lives to ensure that we're continually being restored physically, emotionally, and spiritually. All of nature works in cycles and seasons of productivity and rest. In the climate where I live, we have four distinct seasons. We're surrounded by fertile farmland, so spring is a season for planting. The farmers till the soil and plant their crops. The seeds germinate after the spring rains, and you can watch the new plants growing a little bit higher every day. Summer is a time of heat and humidity, when plants fill out and begin to produce fruit. As fall approaches, the fruit matures and harvest season begins. Once harvest is over, the snow flies and the land rests. During this time, nutrients are returned to the soil so that the whole process can begin again the next year. Without the stillness of winter, the productivity of the other three seasons would be impossible.

Human beings are meant to live in productivity rhythms as well. These rhythms need to find their way into our daily, weekly, and annual routines, or we'll soon find that our bodies start to revolt: immune systems begin to shut down, sleep disorders cause havoc, and depression can set in. Many of the physical ailments that are becoming increasingly common in our day can be traced back to the lack of rest balance in our lives. Stress alone, one of the results of a rest-less life, can be extremely destructive to our psychological and physical well-being over an extended period of time:

There are numerous emotional and physical disorders that have been linked to stress including depression, anxiety, heart attacks, stroke, hypertension, immune system disturbances that increase susceptibility to infections, a host of viral linked disorders ranging from the common cold and herpes to AIDS and certain cancers, as well as autoimmune diseases like rheumatoid arthritis and multiple sclerosis. In addition stress can have direct effects on the skin (rashes, hives, atopic dermatitis, the gastrointestinal system (GERD, peptic ulcer, irritable bowel syndrome, ulcerative colitis) and can contribute to insomnia and degenerative neurological disorders like Parkinson's disease. In fact, it's hard to think of any disease in which stress cannot play an aggravating role or any part of the body that is not affected or. This list will undoubtedly grow as the extensive ramifications of stress are increasingly being appreciated.[12]

We all have seasons when we have to put in extra hours to accomplish a project or meet a deadline. But seasons are meant to have a beginning and an end. When these seasons turn into lifestyles, they become truly unsustainable. We're not made—physically, emotionally, or in any way—for lifestyles of unending busyness without a rest or a break.

Many people have written on the subject of sabbath rest, and I've included a list of works in the Resources

---

[12] "Stress Effects," AIS, accessed November 29, 2018, https://www.stress.org/stress-effects/.

section at the end of the book. If you wish to delve more deeply into the subject, I strongly suggest you get one of the recommended books and dig deeper!

The sabbath principle looks different from person to person. When and how you take time to unplug and rest is somewhat customizable, but it's very important to have down time. If this isn't your current pattern, you may wonder where you'll find time in your week to rest. You won't find the time. A major life priority shift like that requires one to *make* the time. I know this is huge and that, for some, it might be too much to ask, but this ancient pattern for life is just as needed in our day as it was then.

Have you ever wanted the world to stop for a couple of hours so you could catch your breath? The Sabbath is a conscious choice to do just that: to unplug from the world and plug in to the Source of Life, so that your holy pause is not only physically restful, but emotionally and spiritually restorative. Without both components—pausing from your regular pace, and plugging into the source—any attempt at sabbath rhythm will be incomplete.

PAUSING

Although we grew up in very different faith traditions (Assemblies of God and Reformed), my wife and I had similar experiences with the Sabbath (which our families honoured on Sundays) as children. It consisted of a lot of rules about what you couldn't do, taking a mandatory nap, and going to church morning and evening. Sports, loud activities, and other leisure pursuits were out for sure. To our young minds, fun was outlawed. Naps weren't overly welcome either. Sabbath wasn't something we learned to love, but a law we learned to obey. I think it can be both.

Now that I'm older, naps are definitely higher on my list of things to do! I think we have a better understanding today of how differently people are wired. What is restful or renewing to one person may not be to another. For some, gardening is work, but for others, it may be restful and a way to connect with their Creator. For some, reading is a chore, but for others, it restores the soul.

Pausing can take many forms. It's still a good thing to take a nap, or to get more physical rest than one would normally get in one's regular schedule, but it should be combined with joyful, playful activities that give life to your soul. It also shouldn't hinder the second part of sabbath rhythm: plugging in. If our activity makes the Sabbath so busy that we don't have time or energy to connect our hearts with Jesus, then we've simply traded one kind of busyness for another, diminishing the benefits of the Sabbath. The quest to live life differently, with a bottomless cup, will only be realized if we follow the prescription—the seventh day is a sabbath to the Lord, not to ourselves. We all need "me-time" time in which to goof off and do what we want, but in order to tap into God's resources, we need "Jesus-time" too!

These two forms aren't contradictory. Jesus-time isn't some kind of super-spiritual behaviour that must be done on our knees or with hymn music playing in the background. It means bringing Jesus into your God-honouring activity and cherishing His life-giving presence. It means having fellowship, or meaningful connection, with our Saviour in the rhythms of our lives.

Sabbath doesn't have to happen on a particular day of the week either. The New Testament scriptures peel away the rigidity of the Sabbath to make it something that serves us instead of us serving it. Jesus says, "*The Sabbath was made for man, not man for the Sabbath*" (Mark 2:27). Paul writes in Romans 14:5, "*One person considers one day more sacred than another; another considers every day alike. Each of them should be fully convinced in their own mind.*" It's okay to hold one day as a sacred sabbath if that matters to you, but if you want to celebrate Sabbath in a less structured way, that's alright too … as long as you honour it somehow. I work as a pastor, so I'm busy on Sundays. My Sabbath tends to be on Friday, my day off.

As this truth grows in your heart, you'll want more than just a day—you'll want little shots of sabbath throughout your week! Jesus modelled this for us, and it's a healthy part of sabbath rhythm living. Jesus often withdrew for rest and prayer, time to reconnect with the Father. Taking a couple of minutes every hour will make the other fifty-eight minutes more effective. Taking half an hour or an hour every day to fellowship with the Lord will likely improve how you spend the other fifteen waking hours of your day. Taking a couple of days away once or twice a year for a personal retreat will help you focus your heart on hearing the voice of God as He leads you into the next season.

Sabbath rest can be woven into our daily lives and routines in a variety of ways. It just remains to make a plan and do it!

PLUG IN

If you ever access online or phone support for a computer, tablet, router, or other digital device, one of the first questions the technician will ask you is, "Have you tried rebooting it?" Rebooting is an important first step in troubleshooting problems with computers. Over time, the coding information in a computer gets corrupted and starts to malfunction. When you reboot your device, you recalibrate the coding with the original instructions that were built into the device so that it works the way it was intended to.

Sabbath is meant to be for our human coding. Pausing without plugging in misses a major part of what sabbath is all about. Not only do we need to stop, but we need to connect with our Creator so that our hearts can be recalibrated to His heart, our desires with His desires, and our thinking with a kingdom perspective.

Go too long without rebooting your computer and it will begin to act strangely; it will start to freeze up and eventually crash. If we go too long without pausing and plugging in, we begin to malfunction. Our attitude begins to get sour, our interactions with people start to be poisoned by our attitudes, and eventually something will go drastically wrong. Sabbath is a fantastic maintenance strategy for the ongoing health of our lives and relationships.

In Isaiah 58, the prophet addresses the disciplines of fasting and Sabbath-keeping. He talks of how they were misunderstood and misused by the people of Israel to their own harm. Then he speaks from the heart of God, explaining that doing these things right will enhance the effectiveness of his listeners' efforts to change the world:

> *If you keep your feet from breaking the Sabbath and from doing as you please on my holy day, if you call the Sabbath a delight and the Lord's holy day honorable, and if you honour it by not going your own way and not doing as you please or speaking idle words, then you will find your joy in the Lord, and I will cause you to ride in triumph on the heights of the land and to feast on the inheritance of your father Jacob.* (Isaiah 58:13–14)

Sabbath rhythm and the ways in which Jesus wants to train us are keys to ongoing *joy* and *victory*! Who doesn't want those? A large part of our effort in the Christian life is spent in trying to find a way to real joy and victory. We buy books, attend seminars, and go to all kinds of lengths to find joy and victory, all the while neglecting the principles of sabbath rest in our lives. But it isn't working.

Isaiah says that if we honour the Sabbath, we will find our joy in the Lord. We are so desperate for joy, we often look in all the same places as does the world. We think that if we just pour ourselves into our career, we'll find joy in it, or if we make family our top priority and run our kids to every activity in town, we'll find our joy in them.

Maybe if we make enough money, we'll finally be joyful enough to appreciate our lives. Perhaps if we go to enough church meetings and work really hard "for God," we'll find joy in that. But we weren't made to find joy in any of those things, because they don't inherently contain lasting joy. Only our Creator, the source of true joy, contains what our souls long for.

Jesus saw people in His day doing the same thing and said, "I want to show you a new way." This new way involved learning to abide in a place of rest, serving and living from that place of rest, and, in doing so, finding a sustainable strength that would not only prove more effective, but ensure longevity of effectiveness.

PROMISED LAND REST

The writer of Hebrews devotes a significant portion of Chapters Three and Four to the story of Israel's entry into the Promised Land of Canaan. He draws from the story in the Torah and Joshua as well as Psalm 95. The writer must have something important to tell us, but I think we often miss it. It's easy to skim over the sections on the sabbath rest and skip ahead to the end of Chapter Four, which talks about Jesus being our high priest. Now that's good stuff!

But wait a minute … what was he saying about sabbath rest? He explains that God planned this rest for the Israelites as they entered the Promised Land, and they missed it. But if *you* hear His voice today and heed the invitation, you will get to enter in where Israel did not.

Some commentators believe this refers to Heaven, but I would suggest that something more is going on here.

God had promised His people that if they walked in covenant relationship with Him and did not stray to worship and serve other gods, He would bring them into a Promised Land of abundance, to "… *cities you did not build, houses filled with all kinds of good things you did not provide, wells you did not dig, and vineyards and olive groves you did not plant* …" (Deuteronomy 6:10–11). God intended to establish a kingdom where He was king, and His people would be cared for as they learned to live in a covenant relationship of trust with their king. Things didn't work out as God wished, because His people hardened their hearts and constantly rebelled and chose to abandon their covenant with God to worship the gods of the culture around them.

The rest God wished for them was never fully realized. In Psalm 95, as the song writer looks back on the tragic history of Israel and writes a sombre ballad, he says, "*Today, if you hear his voice, do not harden your hearts* …" (Psalm 95:7b–8a, ESV). The writer of Hebrews explains that if Joshua didn't lead his people to enter the rest, but the promise still stands, then you and I can access that promise if we respond to God's invitation. We can live in a place of supernatural provision and experience the grace of God at work in our lives, that producing fruit and having an impact we could never derive from our own efforts. We can live with God as our king, with the resources of His kingdom at our disposal.

This type of sabbath rest goes beyond just a day of the week or a rhythm of our lives, which are both necessary and vital. It's a lifestyle of trust that produces kingdom fruit and effectiveness: "*In repentance and rest is your salvation, in quietness and trust is your strength ...*" (Isaiah 30:15).

> *Even youths grow tired and weary, and young men stumble and fall; but those who hope in the LORD will renew their strength. They will soar on wings like eagles, they will run and not grow weary, they will walk and not be faint.* (Isaiah 40:30–31)

In Matthew 11, Jesus says that if we let Him train us, we will find rest as a place to live from, not just a break from living. We'll find a way to live that will keep us from crashing or burning out, as it provides a supernatural sustaining strength for the journey.

> *For if Joshua had given them rest, God would not have spoken later about another day. There remains, then, a Sabbath-rest for the people of God; for anyone who enters God's rest also rests from their works, just as God did from His. Let us, therefore, make every effort to enter that rest, so that no one will perish by following their example of disobedience.* (Hebrews 4:8–11)

As in Matthew 11, this is an invitation from our God to rest. Notice that the verse says we will rest from our works just as God rested from His. When God "rested" from His work, did He cease to hold the universe together? Of course not! He continued to accomplish all that needed to be done, but from a place of enjoyment, resting in the fruit and blessing of finished work.

In a paradoxical way, when we learn to enter God's rest, we will continue to be fruitful and effective, but not through our own strength, but from the joy of resting in the fruit and blessing of Jesus' finished work. It's no wonder that we're told to make every effort to enter His rest: make every effort to enter an effortless way of life.

In the next chapter, we'll examine this paradoxical life: what it means to work from a place of rest. It's time to trade in our yoke, our burden, for the yoke of Jesus. Then we can do His work in His way.

Questions
FOR REFLECTION AND DISCUSSION

1. What has been your experience with the idea of Sabbath?

2. Do you find it easy to pause in your life rhythm? Why/why not?

3. What does a perfect day of rest look like for you?

4. Where have you often sought for real joy outside of your relationship with God?

5. What helps you connect relationally to Jesus?

6. How do you think you could be more effective or consistent at quality time to connect with Jesus?

7. What do you think is the difference between rest as an activity and rest as a lifestyle?

Chapter Seven
WORKING FROM REST—THE KINGDOM PARADOX

"For my yoke is easy and my burden is light."
(Matthew 11:30)

Are you tired? Worn out? Burned out on religion?
Come to me. Get away with me and you'll recover
your life. I'll show you how to take a real rest. Walk
with me and work with me—watch how I do it.
Learn the unforced rhythms of grace. I won't lay
anything heavy or ill-fitting on you. Keep company
with me and you'll learn to live freely and lightly.
(Matthew 11:28–30, MSG)

I love Eugene Peterson's rendering of our passage in his Bible paraphrase, The Message. He beautifully contrasts the burden of religious, rule-keeping ways of living with the invitation of Jesus to a life of freedom and joy.

Many people in Jesus' day were driven by an obsessive and desperate religious preoccupation with becoming good enough, as are many people of all eras, including many of us today. Because of this, we strive harder and harder to prove to God, to others, and to ourselves that we are worthy of God's favour. This is unfortunate, because God's favour comes by grace, a gift based on the death and resurrection of Jesus on our behalf. But we seem to be hard-wired to seek approval and acceptance based on our performance.

Paul uses the phrase *"elemental spiritual forces of this world"* (Colossians 2:20) to describe our propensity to make and keep rules such as *"Do not handle! Do not taste! Do not touch!"* (Colossians 2:21) as a way of *"restraining* [our] *sensual indulgence"* (Colossians 2:23). But he admits that such measures do nothing to help, because they are void of real power to change the human heart.

I love the way Bono, lead singer of the band U2, puts it in conversation with Michka Assayas:

> It's a mind-blowing concept that the God who created the Universe might be looking for company, a real relationship with people, but the thing that keeps me on my knees is the difference between Grace and Karma …
>
> You see, at the centre of all religions is the idea of Karma. You know, what you put out comes back to you; an eye for an eye, a tooth for a tooth, or in physics—in physical laws—every action is

met by an equal or opposite one. Its clear to me that Karma is at the very heart of the universe. I'm absolutely sure of it.

And yet, along comes this idea called Grace to upend all that "As you reap, so will you sow" stuff. Grace defies reason and logic. Love interrupts, if you like, the consequences of your actions, which in my case is very good news indeed, because I've done a lot of stupid stuff.

That's between me and God. But I'd be in big trouble if Karma was going to finally be my judge … It doesn't excuse my mistakes, but I'm holding out for Grace. I'm holding out that Jesus took my sins onto the Cross because I know who I am, and I hope I don't have to depend on my own religiosity.

The point of the death of Christ is that Christ took on the sins of the world so that what we put out did not come back to us, and that our sinful nature does not reap the obvious death. That's the point. It should keep us humbled … it's not our own good works that get through the gates of heaven …[13]

As Bono suggests, there is something about the way the universe is put together that causes us to expect our behaviour to be weighed to determine whether we pass the big test. Some religions call it Karma, and the Bible

[13] Michka Assayas, *Bono on Bono: Conversations witih Michka Assayas* (New York: Penguin Group, 2005), 226.

says we will reap what we sow. But grace through Jesus says that God no longer looks at us through the lens of our behaviour but through the lens of Jesus' blood shed for us on the cross. I'm not sure we always understand the significance of that.

We have exchanged identities with Jesus. "*God made Him who had no sin to be sin for us, so that in Him we might become the righteousness of God*" (2 Corinthians 5:21). Our beginning place with God is no longer as vile sinners who need to crawl our way up the stairway to Heaven through our efforts, but as redeemed people, adopted sons and daughters, the righteousness of God. It makes a huge difference whether we are working *for* God's approval or *from* God's approval.

Working for God's approval is a deadly treadmill of religious effort by which we continually try to earn what has already been provided for us. Because we're incapable of earning it, we burn ourselves out pursuing the acceptance we long for. We're afraid to risk doing things incorrectly or imperfectly lest we incur his disapproval and judgement. If something fails or isn't working, we just try harder.

Working from God's approval is a lifestyle that begins with the glorious realization that as sons and daughters of the Father, we already have His love and acceptance. Nothing we do can make Him love us more, and nothing we do can make Him love us less. He's crazy about us. Because of that, we can risk doing things for Him, because our acceptance isn't on the line. If we fail, He'll simply smile and say, "Nice try. Have another go at it!" Then He'll set us on our feet again.

James Lawrence in his book *Growing Leaders* compares these two lifestyles, calling the first the Cycle of Grief, and the second, the Cycle of Grace.

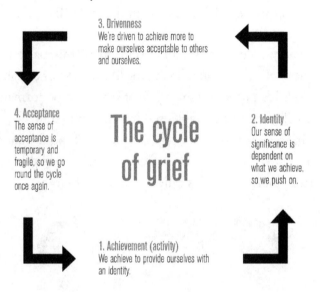

The cycle of grief

3. Drivenness
We're driven to achieve more to make ourselves acceptable to others and ourselves.

4. Acceptance
The sense of acceptance is temporary and fragile, so we go round the cycle once again.

2. Identity
Our sense of significance is dependent on what we achieve, so we push on.

1. Achievement (activity)
We achieve to provide ourselves with an identity.

The above diagram outlines the cycle of grief, which is the cycle from which most of us function.

1. We begin from a place of believing that we're not valued by God unless we achieve something for Him. We work hard to prove ourselves and establish an identity as one loved and approved by God.
2. We accomplish a few things and feel good about ourselves, so we take that as our identity instead of what God says about us.

3. We want more of that feeling of worth because of what we have done, so we feel driven to constantly achieve more.

4. We gain a fragile sense of worth based on the stuff we do for God, but the moment we fail, our identity is threatened, and we begin the cycle all over again.

Many of us have become trapped in this pattern of religious effort instead of living the life of a son or daughter of God. It's a never-ending cycle of slavery to performance that will keep us miserable in our walk with God.

In contrast to this negative cycle of performance, James Lawrence explains that God wants a very different starting place for us. It's called the Cycle of Grace.

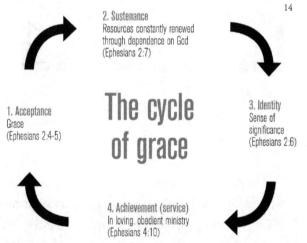

2. Sustenance
Resources constantly renewed through dependence on God (Ephesians 2:7)

The cycle of grace

1. Acceptance
Grace
(Ephesians 2:4-5)

3. Identity
Sense of significance
(Ephesians 2:6)

4. Achievement (service)
In loving, obedient ministry
(Ephesians 4:10)

[14]

This cycle is demonstrated to us by the life of Jesus, and it's the life cycle of a true son or daughter of the Father.

[14] James Lawrence, *Growing Leaders* (Peadbody, MA: Hendrickson Publishers, 2004), 44–45.

When Jesus was about to begin His ministry, he went to John the Baptist to be baptized in water and set apart for the work of God. He had not yet taught a single word, performed any miracles, or trained any disciples. Yet when he came up out of the water, the people there heard the voice of the Father speak over Him, saying, *"You are my Son, whom I love; with you I am well pleased"* (Luke 3:22).

Jesus began His ministry from a place of understanding His approval, acceptance, and identity. He wasn't trying to earn those things; He knew He had them already before He began.

Before I became a dad for the first time, I was really nervous, because I didn't know if I could love a child the way that child needed. But when our baby was born, my heart exploded with love for her, as it did for each of our children. They didn't have to do a thing to earn my love. Even when they threw up on me, or worse, my love for them didn't diminish one bit. That's the way our Father feels about us. We can know His love, His acceptance, and our identity in Him before we do a thing for Him. All of this is possible because of our adoption in Christ. Here's how the second cycle goes:

1. We begin with the Father's acceptance—not for what we've done or not done, but because of Jesus' work accomplished on the cross, and our legal adoption as beloved and chosen children of the Father.

2. God promises us an inheritance of His strength and provision for every challenge and calling, and He puts His Spirit in us that we might know Him.

3. Out of our acceptance by God and our intimacy with Him, we have a rich sense of our identity in Him.

4. Armed with the Father's acceptance, the riches of His resources, and the confidence of our identity in Him, we step out and do the work of ministry that He has called us to do. This brings a sense of achievement that brings even more of a sense of the Father's pleasure, and the cycle begins again.

The Cycle of Grace is a lifestyle rooted and anchored in the truth of what the Father says about us, and it leads to fruitful, abundant life. On the other hand, the Cycle of Grief is a product of the lies that Satan, the enemy of our souls, wants us to believe so that we stay trapped in the captivity of this self-destructive cycle of death. He's the thief that comes to steal, kill, and destroy. He's the author of this desperate religious search for God's approval. As long as we're busy trying to fill our broken souls with our own efforts, we'll never tap into the great strength and authority that comes from finding our identity in God's love and acceptance of us. The enemy will have rendered us ineffective and unproductive.

Even though Jesus knew His identity in the Father, having heard it supernaturally thundered from the heavens when He was in the waters of the Jordan River, Satan attacked Jesus in the desert and called into question His identity, trying to convince Him that He had to prove it. He began each challenge with the words, "If you are the Son of God ..." If Jesus had taken the bait and tried to prove His identity, He would have momentarily lost His anchor in the Father's love for Him and sinned in order to prove Himself.

We fall into this trap all the time. Rather than living from the truth of what God says about us, we fall for the lies the enemy says about us, and we behave in either sinful or religious ways to prove our worth, instead of staying rooted and anchored in the Father's love. This will sap our life and strength and leave us unfruitful, in spite of all of our efforts.

TWO SISTERS, TWO CYCLES

In the Introduction, I said that we'd come back to Mary and Martha. They provide a great example of these two different approaches to life. The story in Luke 10 isn't so much about whether the work needed to be done or not, but the priority Martha put on doing the work versus the priority Mary put on responding to the invitation to be with Jesus.

Is there kingdom work to be done? Yes! There are literally billions of people who need to respond to the gospel of Jesus, and billions of believers need to be discipled and strengthened in their journey. There's always kingdom work to be done; however, you matter more to the Father than do all of your efforts. He doesn't want slaves … He wants sons and daughters. He doesn't want you to earn His favour but to receive it and then go to work, because it's a joy to be part of the family business.

Mary "*sat by the Lord's feet listening to what He said*" (Luke 10:39). This is an expression that meant to learn from a rabbi as a disciple. She had taken the posture of a learner.

Martha, on the other hand, was "*distracted by all the preparations that had to be made*" (Luke 10:40). How often does God see our efforts as a distraction? How often has He extended us an invitation to sit at His feet, to be near Him and learn from Him, and we've claimed to be too busy?

To a performance-oriented achiever, as I've been much of my life, Jesus seems pretty irresponsible, not to mention insensitive to the needs of the moment. Stuff has to get done. If there's time left over, we can "waste" it visiting, but there's a tight ship to run here!

When Martha insists on Jesus' help in corralling her sister, He says, "*Martha, Martha, you are worried and upset about many things, but few things are needed—or indeed only one*" (Luke 10:41–42). He doesn't overtly state what that one thing is, but it's evident from the context that He's referring to the invitation of God. Jesus says, "*Mary has chosen what is better, and it will not be taken away from her*" (v. 42). Mary made a choice. She wasn't being lazy, but she had prioritized receiving from the Master. Martha, on the other hand, had prioritized busyness. We all make choices about our priorities that determine the health of our hearts.

Resentment in serving God isn't unique to Martha, or to me. Many of God's people in scripture felt resentment. Moses cried out to God:

> *I cannot carry all these people by myself; the burden is too heavy for me. If this is how you are going to treat*

me, please go ahead and kill me—if I have found favor in your eyes—and do not let me face my own ruin. (Numbers 11:14–15)

Why did Moses feel like he had to carry the whole nation of Israel? Was that God's intent for him? Of course not! Rather than letting God carry the burden that only He could carry, Moses got the roles confused. The people were demanding a change from the menu of manna. They'd had enough of the same thing every day. They'd tried manna baked, boiled, barbecued, and deep-fried, but no matter how many different recipes they used, it was still manna. They wanted meat. It was one more complaint than Moses could handle, and he freaked!

Moses felt a weight of responsibility that wasn't his, a yoke he wasn't called to carry. He misunderstood God's expectations of him. God didn't ask Moses to feed the people, and He didn't expect him to isolate himself in leadership. To demonstrate this, God had Moses gather seventy elders, and then He anointed them with prophetic power to stand with Moses and help bear the burden of leadership. When Moses complained and asked where the meat was going to come from, God basically said, "Stand back and watch!"

Burnout is a common phenomenon among church leaders, both lay leaders and clergy, because we have a tendency as believers to take on responsibilities that aren't ours and we neglect the invitation to intimacy with God. We prioritize the boardroom over the prayer room, the business of the Father over the pleasure of the Father.

Moses fell into this trap repeatedly, and eventually his resentment in ministry disqualified him from entering the Promised Land. He didn't finish as well as he could have because he didn't maintain his earlier priority of pursuing the face of God.

We shouldn't be too hard on Moses, though. It's easy to start out with a burning zeal to know God and to minister out of the fire and passion that comes from walking with Him, but then to slip into professionalism. We learn how to do a few things, discover that we can write a sermon, or lead a meeting, or even share the gospel without a lot of prayer or dependence on God. What used to keep us clinging to Jesus is now just a job. Now we have to be intentional about intimacy with God, because we can kind of fake it without Him. That's a scary place to be.

Rather than ministering out of an intimacy with God, we minister out of our organizational skills, or the strength of our charisma or personality. We trust in our wisdom and past successes instead of living on the leading edge with the Holy Spirit. The longer we do this, the more we take responsibility for things only God can do, and the less effective our ministry becomes. Then we blame God for not coming through for us, and our identity, which has become wrapped up in what we do for God instead of what He has done for us, takes a hit. We're failing, so God must not be pleased. So we try harder. It's an ugly downward spiral, as depicted by the cycle of grief.

Just like we can either work for God's acceptance or from His acceptance, we can work for His rest or from His rest. We rest in His acceptance, His blessing, His peace, and His provision. By doing so, we live in the constant realization that He is God, and we are not, and that we aren't responsible for the things He has promised to do. We simply trust Him and do what He asks of us. This is the relationship of dependence and trust that Jesus walked in with the Father, and it's the key to His strength and peace in all circumstances.

This is why we can live and minister with a bottomless cup, because it's not our strength being exerted in the work of ministry. When we do it right, it's the strength of Christ working in and through us. When speaking about his calling to grow and disciple believers in Christ, Paul says, "*For this I toil, struggling with all his energy that he powerfully works in me*" (Colossians 1:29, ESV). Do we work for God? Do we toil for His kingdom? Yes, but we do it with the energy of Christ that He powerfully works in us. If we're burnt out, if we're empty and drained, then we're doing something wrong. I've been there many times and have heard Jesus whisper to my spirit, "Come to me, all you who are weary and burdened ..."

When the writer of Hebrews tells us to make every effort to enter the sabbath rest, I believe he's telling us to enter into the Promised Land of faith and confidence in the finished work of Christ, in the unfailing love of the Father, and in the assurance that our confidence is not in our ability but the presence and power of the Holy Spirit to accomplish the works of God through our lives. When we can truly do this, we will enter a season of our

Christian life in which the work of the kingdom isn't a burden but a joy.

We won't over-extend ourselves, because we won't feel obligated to do what only God can do. We won't burn out, because we won't be driven to prove something to others or ourselves. We won't be consumed with gaining the acceptance or approval of our Heavenly Father, but we'll daily rejoice in the fact that it's already ours. This will be ours if we learn to function from the cycle of grace and from a place of Promised Land rest! We do not work *in order* to be loved and saved, but we work *because* we are loved and saved. What a difference!

Questions
FOR REFLECTION AND DISCUSSION

1. On a scale of 1 to 10, how would you rate your level of understanding that you are loved by God? (1 = a very low understanding, 10 = you never question it)

2. What do you think is your biggest obstacle to accepting the love of God?

3. Do you relate more closely to Mary or to Martha in the story from the Gospel of Luke? In what way?

4. What would be the biggest difference between a life lived in the Cycle of Grief and one lived in the Cycle of Grace?

5. Which cycle more closely describes your life right now? If you need to change cycles, where do you think you might start today?

6. How can we pray for you to make this change?

Conclusion

THE REAL STORY

In the Introduction, I indicated that I write this book with questionable credentials and not as one who has the whole thing figured out yet. I'm not in bad of company when I say that. The apostle Paul said, *"Not that I have already obtained all this, or have already arrived at my goal, but I press on to take hold of that for which Christ Jesus took hold of me"* (Philippians 3:12).

In twenty-five years of full-time pastoral ministry, my wife and I have each been close to, or in, burnout on more than one occasion. We are passionate and zealous people, but sometimes our passion has been spent on things God didn't call us to do. Sometimes we were more interested in proving to God how good we were, or to others how important we were, than we were in resting humbly in what Jesus had already done.

Learning the "unforced rhythms of grace" has been a progressive and growing journey that we're still on. We consider ourselves lifetime learners of the yoke of Jesus. Sometimes we have to re-learn stuff we thought we'd gotten down pat already. The old lies creep in, and we forget the delight the Father has in us, and the resources He has already made available to us, and we begin striving in our strength to please Him.

I believe this lifestyle that Jesus invites us to is available and achievable. If it wasn't, Jesus wouldn't have invited us. He's not unkind or sadistic. I believe this is the message of grace that runs through the scriptures, both Old and New Testaments. It's also a major key to living in the Kingdom of God.

Living religiously means striving to do what only God can truly do by using fleshly, human effort for fleshly, human motives. It's built on a faulty understanding of our identity that believes we only have value to God when we perform for Him and succeed in the world's eyes.

Living in the kingdom means to submit your life to the King, to follow His leading, and to do what He asks you to do, using the resources He has already provided and then giving Him the glory when you succeed. It's built on a healthy understanding of our identity as chosen and adopted sons/daughters of God because of Jesus. We *are* loved, so all that we do is done as a thank offering to bring joy and delight to our Heavenly Father.

One path leads to a kind of spiritual death—a form of godliness that denies its power (2 Timothy 3:5). The other leads to the fruit of the kingdom: righteousness, peace, and joy in the Holy Spirit (Romans 14:19).

The New Testament gospels provide a clear picture of these two paths as the scribes and Pharisees are contrasted with Jesus. These men are the favourite punching bags of most Bible teachers, but we have to ask if we look more like the ministry of Jesus than they did.

The Scribes and Pharisees:

- were intensely committed to biblical authority
- stood in strong opposition to changes in the culture and morality brought about by the lifestyles and beliefs of the pagans in the society around them
- were more committed to the status quo than to innovation
- were territorial and protectionist when it came to losing influence in society
- were perceived as having little moral authority because of the lack of congruence between what they taught and what they did
- resorted to manipulation, control, and guilt to keep people under the influence of their authority
- talked about the power of God, but never saw it manifested through their ministry
- were more afraid of losing public support than of doing wrong
- left people tired, burnt out, and miserable
- loved position and titles more than they loved people

Jesus

- was more concerned about the scriptures leading us into a relationship with the author
- was more concerned that those who know God live as a light than lead a protest

- was happy to shake up the status quo for the sake of reaching people who needed a message of hope
- was not threatened by other preachers or messengers
- was perceived as speaking with more authority than any other teacher because of the congruence between His life and message
- clearly manifested the power of God in and through His life on a daily basis
- never tailored His message for public support
- caused people to joyfully and willingly lay down their lives
- laid down every title and position in order to pursue people

Does your life, ministry, or church look more like the Scribes and Pharisees, or more like the ministry of Jesus? One is religious, the other is the Kingdom of God. I think we're presumptuous to not admit that there is some Pharisee in all of us.

I wish I could say that I've always done ministry from a kingdom mindset, but sometimes there's way too much of me mixed in. But I am learning and growing, and I think I can say that I'm living a kingdom lifestyle more regularly.

If you're tired of a Pharisee-like, religious existence that talks a good talk but is largely void of joy and real effectiveness, and leaves you worn out, why not listen to Jesus' invitation? He will:

- give you a shelter where you can rest and restore your soul;
- take you in as a disciple, a trainee in His way of life and ministry;
- show you how to tune your heart to the gentle leading of the Spirit, to step out in faith, trusting in the power of Heaven at your disposal;
- enable you to enter a Promised Land existence, where you live daily from a place of inner rest and peace;
- make your service to God the greatest joy of your life rather than a heavy burden of fear and guilt.

The best thing about the bottomless cup Jesus offers is that it's free.

"Praise be to the God and Father of our Lord Jesus Christ, who has blessed us in the heavenly realms with every spiritual blessing in Christ" (Ephesians 1:3).

Epilogue

RESOURCES FOR LIVING WITH A BOTTOMLESS CUP

CHAPTER ONE SUGGESTED RESOURCES

Some resources to help us see that Jesus came to give a revelation of the Father to us that is different than our religious ideas of God:

Philip Yancey, *The Jesus I Never Knew* (Grand Rapids, MI: 1995).

Philip Yancey helps us come to grips with who Jesus really was. We often try to remake Him according to our own cultural values. But when we get to know the real Jesus of the Bible in a fresh way, we're challenged to see how the Father is revealed in Him.

CHAPTER TWO SUGGESTED RESOURCES

Some resources to help you discover in a fresh way that the gospel is an invitation from a God who loves you:

Brennan Manning, *The Ragamuffin Gospel* (Colorado Springs: Multnomah, 2005).

Brennan Manning brings out the beauty of the gospel as being for those who need it, not those who already have life figured out. Through his own struggles and failures, he rediscovered the reality and power of the good news.

Steve McVey, *A Divine Invitation* (Atlanta: Gracewalk Resources, 2008).

With a biblical message of grace, Steve helps us to see the gospel as an invitation to a life in which we rely not on what we can produce by human effort, but on the one who works *in* us to accomplish His great purpose.

Richard Rohr with Mike Morell, *The Divine Dance: The Trinity and Your Transformation* (New Kensington, PA: Whitaker House, 2016).

Richard Rohr, in a very thought provoking and poetic way, introduces us to the perichoresis, the rhythm of the Trinity that, in Christ, invites all of humanity and all of creation to join in the community of God.

Gary Thomas, *Sacred Pathways: Discover Your Soul's Path to God*, (Grand Rapids, MI: Zondervan, 1996).

Your way of connecting to God is as unique as you are. It could be through prayer, music, serving, study, or other actions. Therefore, God's invitation to you is a unique invitation. This book will help you discover how you might best connect to Him.

CHAPTER THREE SUGGESTED RESOURCES

Resources for the tired, the weary, the burnt out. Jesus is our refuge, but how can we find hope in Him when our religious experience has contributed to our fatigue?

Ian Morgan Cron, *Chasing Francis: A Pilgrim's Tale* (Grand Rapids, MI: Zondervan, 2013).

After becoming burned out and losing his grip on faith, a pastor takes a sabbatical and goes on a journey of rediscovering the core of the faith in unlikely places.

Dr. Grant Mullen, M.D., *Emotionally Free, A Prescription for Healing Body, Soul and Spirit* (Mustang, OK: Tate Publishing, 2013).

Dr. Mullen unpacks the reality of mental illness and depression for the Christian and how our physical, emotional, and spiritual selves are interconnected, as is the healing process.

Peter Scazzero, *Emotionally Healthy Church*, (Grand Rapids, MI: Zondervan, 2010).

Peter and his wife Gerri had been doing church as usual, and it was killing them and their family. Something had to change, and the change that came revolutionized their lives—and their church.

CHAPTER FOUR SUGGESTED RESOURCES

Some resources to help you become a more faithful disciple of Jesus, to sit at his feet and learn how to live the life He calls you to live:

Dietrich Bonhoeffer, *The Cost of Discipleship* (New York, NY: Touchstone, 1959).

In this important work, Bonhoeffer uses the teachings of Jesus in the Sermon on the Mount to show us the depth of His call to commitment and what it really means to become His disciple.

Dallas Willard, *The Divine Conspiracy: Rediscovering our Hidden Life in God* (New York, NY: HarperCollins, 1998).

Dallas Willard also uses the Sermon on the Mount in this equally significant book to show us how we are to reorient our lives as Christians around the teachings and life of Jesus.

CHAPTER FIVE SUGGESTED RESOURCES

Some resources to help you learn to live in God's presence more consistently and to hear and be led by His voice more clearly.

Gene Edwards, *100 Days in the Secret Place* (Shippensburg, PA: Destiny Image, 2015).

Gene Edwards pulls together some beautiful writings from three seventeenth century Christian mystics who knew how to connect with God. Their writings are presented in bite-sized daily readings that will help you grow in your understanding of how to *be* with God.

Brad Jersak, *Can You Hear Me?: Tuning in to the God Who Speaks*, (Abbotsford, BC: Fresh Wid Press, 2003).

Brad provides practical teaching on how to tune our hearts to the frequency of God's voice. If we're to be led by Jesus, we need to learn to hear Him speak!

Brother Lawrence, *The Practice of the Presence of God* (Brewster, MA: Paraclete Press, 2010).

This classic brings us into conversation with a simple monk who learned how to dwell in God's presence in the midst of his mundane daily tasks.

Mark and Patti Virkler, *4 Keys to Hearing God's Voice* (Shippensburg, PA: Destiny Image Publishers, 2010).

Mark and Patti have been teaching on this subject for years, helping people learn biblically balanced and wise ways to hear God speak to them and lead their lives.

Bruce Wilkinson, *Secrets of the Vine* (Sisters, OR: Multnomah Press, 2001).

In this little book, Bruce Wilkinson shares his experience of trying to abide in the presence of God through his own efforts, and then the difference it made to be plugged into the vine itself.

CHAPTER SIX SUGGESTED RESOURCES

In our busy world, we have lost the art of sabbath and healthy rhythms of rest, restoration, and work. Here are some resources that may help you rediscover the importance and power of this principle in your life.

Randy Frazee, *Making Room for Life* (Grand Rapids, MI: Zondervan, 2003).

Randy Frazee challenges us to examine the pace of our lives in Western culture and how it is destroying our families and our emotional and relational core. He gives practical suggestions for slowing down our pace to make room for God and others.

Mark Buchanan, *The Rest of God* (Nashville, TN: Thomas Nelson, 2006).

Mark Buchanan uses a play on words to demonstrate that there is more to God than most of us realize, and the rest is the rest. He wants us to be restored in His presence.

Mark Banyard, *Entering the Sabbath Rest* (Kingdom Advance Ministries, 2004).

Mark Banyard takes us deeper into the meaning of entering the sabbath rest talked about in the book of Hebrews. Currently only available in eBook form.

Alex Soojung-Kim Pang, *Rest: Why You Get More Done When You Work Less* (New York, NY: Basic Books, 2016).

This book deals with the science of our bodies needing a regular cycle of rest. It's not a Christian book, but it clearly shows us how sabbath is built into our human physiology.

Peter Scazzero, *Emotionally Healthy Spirituality* (Nashville, TN: Thomas Nelson, 2006).

This book is a *must* for those serious about living differently. It also can be studied as a course with workbooks. Peter Scazzero demonstrates that many of our emotional and life patterns can be unhealthy, and we wonder why parts of our lives seem unchanged even though we've been disciples for so long.

CHAPTER SEVEN SUGGESTED RESOURCES

How do we stop striving in our own strength and begin functioning out of a place of rest and trust? These resources are intended to help you grow in this area.

Bill Gillham, *Lifetime Guarantee* (Eugene, OR: Harvest House, 1993).

As a professor, counsellor, and radio host, Gillham heard countless stories of people who tried to live the Christian life but repeatedly failed. Then he realized that only one person can live like Christ—Jesus Himself—and that He wants to live His life through each and every believer.

Bill Johnson, *Strengthen Yourself in the Lord* (Shippensburg, PA: Destiny Image, 2007).

Bill Johnson helps us understand that we were never meant to do the work of God in our own strength, but we can find ongoing renewal from the life of Jesus *in* us.

Steve McVey, *Grace Walk* (Eugene, OR: Harvest House, 1995).

Steve shares from personal experience how a legalistic and overly religious approach to life almost destroyed him, and how he learned that the Christian life is about learning to let Jesus live His life through us.

CPSIA information can be obtained
at www.ICGtesting.com
Printed in the USA
LVHW032342011019
632931LV00014B/420/P